# INHERITORS

# INHERITORS

## A PLAY IN THREE ACTS

BY

SUSAN GLASPELL

BOSTON
SMALL, MAYNARD & COMPANY
PUBLISHERS

# INHERITORS
## A PLAY IN THREE ACTS

BY

## SUSAN GLASPELL

First Performed by the Provincetown Players
New York City, March 21, 1921

## ORIGINAL CAST

| | |
|---|---|
| Smith . . . . . . . . . . . . | A. K. MILLER |
| Grandmother, *Silas Morton's Mother* . . . . . . . . . . . . | BLANCHE HAYS |
| Felix Fejevary, 1st . . . . . | ARNOLD SCHWARZ |
| Silas Morton . . . . . . . | GEORGE CRAM COOK |
| Felix, *Son of Felix Fejevary, 1st* . | WILLIAM RAINEY |
| Senator Lewis, *A State Senator* . | ALAN McATEER |
| Horace, *Son of Felix Fejevary, 2nd* . | ANDREW FRASER |
| Doris ⎫ *College Girls* . . . ⎧ | JEANNIE BEGG |
| Fussie ⎭ ⎩ | EMILY TAFT |
| Madeline Fejevary Morton . . . . | ANN HARDING |
| Aunt Isabel, *Wife of Felix Fejevary, 2nd* . . . . . . . . . . . | ELIZABETH BROWN |
| Harry, *A Student Clerk* . . . . . | DONN MILLER |
| Professor Holden . . . . . . . | JAMES LIGHT |
| Ira Morton, *Son of Silas Morton* . | JASPER DEETER |
| Emil Johnson . . . . . . . . | HAROLD McGEE |

# INHERITORS

# INHERITORS

## ACT ONE

SCENE: *Sitting-room of the Morton's farmhouse in the middle west—on the rolling prairie just back from the Mississippi. A room that has been long and comfortably lived in, and showing that first-hand contact with materials which was pioneer life. The hospitable table was made on the place—well and strongly made; there are braided rugs, and the wooden chairs have patchwork cushions. There is a corner closet—left rear. A picture of Abraham Lincoln. On the floor a home-made toy boat. At rise of curtain there are on the stage an old woman and a young man.* GRANDMOTHER MORTON *is in her rocking-chair near the open door, facing left. On both sides of door are windows, looking out on a generous land. She has a sewing basket and is patching a boy's pants. She is very old. Her hands tremble. Her spirit remembers the days of her strength.*

SMITH *has just come in and, hat in hand, is standing by the table. This was lived in the year 1879, afternoon of Fourth of July.*

### SMITH

But the celebration was over two hours ago.

### GRANDMOTHER

Oh, celebration, that's just the beginning of it. Might as well set down. When them boys that fought together all get in one square—they have to swap stories all over again. That's the worst of a war—you have to go on hearing about it so long. Here it is—1879—and we haven't taken Gettysburg yet. Well, it was the same way with the war of 1832.

### SMITH

[*Who is now seated at the table.*] The war of 1832?

### GRANDMOTHER

News to you that we had a war with the Indians?

### SMITH

That's right—the Blackhawk war. I've heard of it.

### GRANDMOTHER

Heard of it!

### SMITH

Were your men in that war?

### GRANDMOTHER

I was in that war. I threw an Indian in the cellar and stood on the door. I was heavier then.

### SMITH

Those were stirring times.

### GRANDMOTHER

More stirring than you'll ever see. This war—Lincoln's war—it's all a cut and dried business now. We used to fight with anything we could lay hands on—dish water—whatever was handy.

### SMITH

I guess you believe the saying that the only good Indian is a dead Indian.

### GRANDMOTHER

I dunno. We roiled them up considerable. They was mostly friendly when let be. Didn't want to give up their land—but I've noticed something of the same nature in white folks.

### SMITH

Your son has—something of that nature, hasn't he?

### GRANDMOTHER

He's not keen to sell. Why should he? It'll never be worth less.

### SMITH

But since he has more land than any man can use, and if he gets his price—

### GRANDMOTHER

That what you've come to talk to him about?

### SMITH

I—yes.

### GRANDMOTHER

Well, you're not the first. Many a man older than you has come to argue it.

### SMITH

[*Smiling.*] They thought they'd try a young one.

### GRANDMOTHER

Some one that knew him thought that up. Silas'd help a young one if he could. What is it you're set on buying?

SMITH

Oh, I don't know that we're set on buying anything. If we could have the hill [*Looking off to the right*] at a fair price—

GRANDMOTHER

The hill above the town? Silas'd rather sell me and the cat.

SMITH

But what's he going to do with it?

GRANDMOTHER
Maybe he's going to climb it once a week.

SMITH

But if the development of the town demands its use—

GRANDMOTHER

[*Smiling.*] You the development of the town?

SMITH

I represent it. This town has been growing so fast—

GRANDMOTHER

This town began to grow the day I got here.

SMITH

You—you began it?

GRANDMOTHER

My husband and I began it—and our baby Silas.

SMITH

When was that?

GRANDMOTHER

1820, that was.

SMITH

And—you mean you were here all alone?

GRANDMOTHER

No, we weren't alone. We had the Owens ten miles down the river.

SMITH

But how did you get here?

GRANDMOTHER

Got here in a wagon, how do you s'pose? [*Gayly*] Think we flew?

SMITH

But wasn't it unsafe?

GRANDMOTHER

Them set on safety staid back in Ohio.

SMITH

But one family! I should think the Indians would have wiped you out.

GRANDMOTHER

The way they wiped us out was to bring fish and corn. We'd have starved to death that first winter hadn't been for the Indians.

### SMITH

But if they were such good neighbors—why did you throw dish water at them?

### GRANDMOTHER

That was after other white folks had roiled them up—white folks that didn't know how to treat 'em. This very land—land you want to buy—was the land they loved—Blackhawk and his Indians. They came here for their games. This was where their fathers—as they called 'em—were buried. I've seen my husband and Blackhawk climb that hill together. [*A backward point right.*] He used to love that hill—Blackhawk. He talked how the red man and the white man could live together. But poor old Blackhawk—what he didn't know was how many white man there was. After the war—when he was beaten but not conquered in his heart—they took him east—Washington, Philadelphia, New York—and when he saw the white man's cities—it was a different Indian came back. He just let his heart break without ever turning a hand.

### SMITH

But we paid them for their lands. [*She looks at him.*] Paid them something.

### GRANDMOTHER

Something. For fifteen million acres of this Mississippi Valley land—best on this globe, we paid two thousand two hundred and thirty-four dollars and fifty cents, and promised to deliver annually goods to the value of one thousand dollars. Not a fancy price—even for them days.

[*Children's voices are heard outside.  She leans forward and looks through the door, left.*]  Ira! Let that cat be!

## SMITH

[*Looking from the window.*]  These, I suppose, are your grandchildren?

## GRANDMOTHER

The boy's my grandson.  The little girl is Madeline Fejevary—Mr. Fejevary's youngest child.

## SMITH

The Fejevary place adjoins on this side?
[*Pointing right, down.*

## GRANDMOTHER

Yes.  We've been neighbors ever since the Fejevarys came here from Hungary after 1848.  He was a count at home—and he's a man of learning.  But he was a refugee because he fought for freedom in his country.  Nothing Silas could do for him was too good.  Silas sets great store by learning—and freedom.

## SMITH

[*Thinking of his own project, looking off toward the hill—the hill is not seen from the front.*]  I suppose then Mr. Fejevary has great influence with your son?

## GRANDMOTHER

More 'an anybody.  Silas thinks 'twas a great thing for our family to have a family like theirs next place to.  Well—so 'twas, for we've had no time for the things their family was brought up in.  Old Mrs. Fejevary [*with her shrewd smile*]—she weren't stuck up—but she did have an awful ladylike way of feeding the chickens. Silas thinks—oh my son has all kinds of notions—though a harder worker never found his bed at night.

### SMITH

And Mr. Fejevary—is he a veteran too?

### GRANDMOTHER

[*Dryly.*] You don't seem to know these parts well—for one that's all stirred up about the development of the town. Yes—Felix Fejevary and Silas Morton went off together, down that road [*motioning with her hand, right*]—when them of their age was wanted. Fejevary came back with one arm less than he went with. Silas brought home everything he took—and something he didn't. Rheumatiz. So now they set more store by each other 'an ever. Seems nothing draws men together like killing other men. [*A boy's voice teasingly imitating a cat.*] Madeline, make Ira let that cat be. [*A whoop from the girl—a boy's whoop.*] [*Looking.*] There they go, off for the creek. If they set in it—[*Seems about to call after them, gives this up.*] Well, they're not the first.

[*Rather dreams over this.*

### SMITH

You must feel as if you pretty near owned this country.

### GRANDMOTHER

We worked. A country don't make itself. When the sun was up we were up, and when the sun went

down we didn't. [*As if this renews the self of those days.*] Here—let me set out something for you to eat.
[*Gets up with difficulty.*

### SMITH

Oh, no, please—never mind. I had something in town before I came out.

### GRANDMOTHER

Dunno as that's any reason you shouldn't have something here.

> [*She goes off, right; he stands at the
> door, looking toward the hill until she
> returns with a glass of milk, a plate
> of cookies.*

### SMITH

Well, this looks good.

### GRANDMOTHER

I've fed a lot of folks—take it by and large. I didn't care how many I had to feed in the daytime—what's ten or fifteen more when you're up and around. But to *get* up—after sixteen hours on your feet—*I* was willin', but my bones complained some.

### SMITH

But did you—keep a tavern?

### GRANDMOTHER

Keep a tavern? I guess we did. Every house is a tavern when houses are sparse. You think the way to settle a country is to go on ahead and build hotels?

That's all you folks know. Why, I never went to bed without leaving something on the stove for the new ones that might be coming. And we never went away from home without seein' there was aplenty for them that might stop.

### SMITH

They'd come right in and take your food?

### GRANDMOTHER

What else could they do? There was a woman I always wanted to know. She made a kind of bread I never had before—and left aplenty for our supper when we got back with the ducks and berries. And she left the kitchen handier than it had ever been. I often wondered about her—where she came from, and where she went. [*As she dreams over this there is laughing and talking at the side of the house.*] There come the boys.

> [MR. FEJEVARY *comes in, followed by* SILAS MORTON. *They are men not far from sixty, wearing their army uniforms, carrying the muskets they used in the parade.* FEJEVARY *has a lean, distinguished face, his dark eyes are penetrating and rather wistful. The left sleeve of his old uniform is empty.* SILAS MORTON *is a strong man who has borne the burden of the land, and not for himself alone—the pioneer. Seeing the stranger, he sets his musket against the wall and holds out his hand to him, as* MR. FEJEVARY *goes up to* GRANDMOTHER MORTON.

SILAS

How'do, stranger?

FEJEVARY

And how are you today, Mrs. Morton?

GRANDMOTHER

I'm not abed—and don't expect to be.

SILAS

[*Letting go one of the balloons he has bought.*]
Where's Ira? And Madeline?

GRANDMOTHER

Mr. Fejevary's Delia brought them home with her.
They've gone down to dam the creek, I guess. This
young man's been waiting to see you, Silas.

SMITH

Yes, I wanted to have a little talk with you.

SILAS

Well, why not? [*He is tying the gay balloons to his
gun, then as he talks, hangs his hat in the corner closet.*]
We've been having a little talk ourselves. Mother, Nat
Rice was there. I've not seen Nat Rice since the day
we had to leave him on the road with his torn leg—him
cursing like a pirate. I wanted to bring him home, but
he had to go back to Chicago. His wife's dead, mother.

GRANDMOTHER

Well, I guess she's not sorry.

SILAS

Why, mother.

GRANDMOTHER

"Why, mother." Nat Rice is a mean, stingy, complaining man—his leg notwithstanding. Where'd you leave the folks?

SILAS

Oh—scattered around. Everybody visitin' with anybody that'll visit with them. Wish you could have gone.

GRANDMOTHER

I've heard it all. [*To* FEJEVARY.] Your folks well?

FEJEVARY

All well, Mrs. Morton. And my boy Felix is home. He'll stop in here to see you by and by.

SILAS

Oh, he's a fine looking boy, mother. And think of what he knows! [*Cordially including the young man.*] Mr. Fejevary's son has been to Harvard College.

SMITH

Well, well—quite a trip. Well, Mr. Morton, I hope this is not a bad time for me to—present a little matter to you?

SILAS

[*Genially.*] That depends, of course, on what you're going to present. [*Attracted by a sound outside.*] Mind if I present a little matter to your horse? Like to uncheck him so's he can get a bite o' grass.

SMITH

Why—yes. I suppose he would like that.

#### Silas

[*Going out.*] You bet he'd like it. Wouldn't you, old boy?

#### Smith

Your son is fond of animals.

#### Grandmother

Lots of people's fond of 'em—and good to 'em. Silas—I dunno, it's as if he was that animal.

#### Fejevary

He has imagination.

#### Grandmother

[*With surprise.*] Think so?

#### Silas

[*Returning and sitting down at the table by the young man.*] Now, what's in your mind, my boy?

#### Smith

This town is growing very fast, Mr. Morton.

#### Silas

Yes. [*Slyly—with humor.*] I know that.

#### Smith

I presume you, as one of the early settlers—as in fact a son of the earliest settler, feel a certain responsibility about the welfare of—

#### Silas

I haven't got it in mind to do the town a bit of harm. So—what's your point?

### SMITH

More people—more homes. And homes must be in
the healthiest places—the—the most beautiful places.
Isn't it true, Mr. Fejevary, that it means a great deal to
people to have a beautiful outlook from their homes?
A—well, an expanse.

### SILAS

What is it they want to buy—these fellows that are
figuring on making something out of—expanse? [*A
gesture for expanse, then a reassuring gesture.*]   It's
all right, but—just what is it?

### SMITH

I am prepared to make you an offer—a gilt-edged
offer for that [*pointing toward it*] hill above the town.

### SILAS

[*Shaking his head—with the smile of the strong man
who is a dreamer.*]   The hill is not for sale.

### SMITH

But wouldn't you consider a—particularly good offer,
Mr. Morton?
               [SILAS, *who has turned so he can look out
               at the hill, slowly shakes his head.*

### SMITH

Do you quite feel you have the right—the moral right
to hold it?

### SILAS

It's not for myself I'm holding it.

SMITH

Oh,—for the children?

SILAS

Yes, the children.

SMITH

But—if you'll excuse me—there are other invest-ments might do the children even more good.

SILAS

This seems to me—the best investment.

SMITH

But after all there are other people's children to con-sider.

SILAS

Yes, I know. That's it.

SMITH

I wonder if I unaerstand you, Mr. Morton?

SILAS

[*Kindly.*] I don't believe you do. I don't see how you could. And I can't explain myself just now. So— the hill is not for sale. I'm not making anybody home-less. There's land enough for all—all sides round. But the hill—

SMITH

[*Rising.*] Is yours.

SILAS

You'll see.

SMITH

I am prepared to offer you—

SILAS

You're not prepared to offer me anything I'd consider alongside what I am considering. So—I wish you good luck in your business undertakings.

SMITH

orry—you won't let us try to help the town.

SILAS

Don't sit up nights worrying about my chokin' the town.

SMITH

We could make you a rich man, Mr. Morton. Do you think what you have in mind will make you so much richer?

SILAS

Much richer.

SMITH

Well, good-bye. Good day, sir. Good day, ma'am.

SILAS

[*Following him to the door.*] Nice horse you've got.

SMITH

Yes, seems all right.

[SILAS *stands in the doorway and looks off at the hill.*

GRANDMOTHER

What are you going to do with the hill, Silas?

SILAS

After I get a little glass of wine—to celebrate Felix and me being here instead of farther south—I'd like to tell you what I want for the hill. [*To Fejevary rather bashfully.*] I've been wanting to tell you.

FEJEVARY

I want to know.

SILAS

[*Getting the wine from the closet.*] Just a little something to show our gratitude with.

[*Goes off right for glasses.*

GRANDMOTHER

I dunno. Maybe it'd be better to sell the hill—while they're anxious.

FEJEVARY

He seems to have another plan for it.

GRANDMOTHER

Yes. Well, I hope the other plan does bring him something. Silas has worked—all the days of his life.

FEJEVARY

I know.

GRANDMOTHER

You don't know the hull of it. But I know. [*Rather to herself.*] Know too well to think about it.

#### Grandmother

[*As* Silas *returns.*]    I'll get more cookies.

#### Silas

I'll get them, mother.

#### Grandmother

Get 'em myself.    Pity if a woman can't set out her own cookies.

#### Silas

[*Seeing how hard it is for her.*]    I wish mother would let us do things for her.

#### Fejevary

That strength is a flame frailness can't put out.    It's a great thing for us to have her,—this touch with the life behind us.

#### Silas

Yes.    And it's a great thing for us to have you—who can see those things and say them.    What a lot I'd 'a'missed if I hadn't had what you've seen.

#### Fejevary

Oh, you only think that because you've got to be generous.

#### Silas

I'm not generous.    *I'm* seeing something now.    Something about you.    I've been thinking of it a good deal lately—it's got something to do with—with the hill. I've been thinkin' what it's meant all these years to have a family like yours next place to.    They did something pretty nice for the corn belt when they drove you out of Hungary. Funny—how things don't end the way they begin. I mean, what begins don't end. It's another thing ends. Set out to do something for your own country—and maybe you don't quite do the thing you set out to do—

### FEJEVARY

No.

### SILAS

But do something for a country a long way off.

### FEJEVARY

I'm afraid I've not done much for any country.

### SILAS

[*Brusquely.*] Where's your left arm—may I be so bold as to inquire? Though your left arm's nothing alongside—what can't be measured.

### FEJEVARY

When I think of what I dreamed as a young man— it seems to me my life has failed.

### SILAS

[*Raising his glass.*] Well, if your life's failed—I like failure

> [*Grandmother Morton returns with her cookies.*

### GRANDMOTHER

There's two kinds—Mr. Fejevary. These have seeds in 'em.

FEJEVARY

Thank you. I'll try a seed cookie first.

SILAS

Mother, you'll have a little glass of wine?

GRANDMOTHER

I don't need wine.

SILAS

Well, I don't know as we need it.

GRANDMOTHER

No, I don't know as you do. But I didn't go to war.

FEJEVARY

Then have a little wine to celebrate that.

GRANDMOTHER

Well, just a mite to warm me up. Not that it's cold. [*Fejevary brings it to her, and the cookies.*] The Indians used to like cookies. I was talking to that young whippersnapper about the Indians. One time I saw an Indian watching me from a bush. [*Points.*] Right out there. I was never afraid of Indians when you could see the whole of em—but when you could see nothin' but their bright eyes—movin' through leaves—I declare they made me nervous. After he'd been there an hour I couldn't seem to put my mind on my work. So I thought, Red or White, a man's a man—I'll take him some cookies.

FEJEVARY

It succeeded?

### Grandmother

So well that those leaves had eyes next day. But he brought me a fish to trade. He was a nice boy.

### Silas

Probably we killed him.

### Grandmother

I dunno. Maybe he killed us. Will Owens' family was massacred just after this. Like as not my cookie Indian helped out there. Something kind of uncertain about the Indians.

### Silas

I guess they found something kind of uncertain about us.

### Grandmother

Six o' one and half a dozen of another. Usually is.

### Silas

[*To* Fejevary.] I wonder if I'm wrong. You see, I never went to school—

### Grandmother

I don't know why you say that, Silas. There was two winters you went to school.

### Silas

Yes, mother, and I'm glad I did, for I learned to read there, and I liked the geography globe. It made the earth so nice to think about. And one day the teacher told us all about the stars, and I had that to think of when I was driving at night. The other boys didn't believe it was so. But I knew it was so! But I mean school—the way Mr. Fejevary went to school. He went to universities. In his own countries—in other countries. All the things men have found out, the wisest and finest things men have thought since first they began to think—all that was put before him.

FEJEVARY

[*With a gentle smile.*] I fear I left a good deal of it untouched.

SILAS

You took aplenty. Tell in your eyes you've thought lots about what's been thought. And that's what I was setting out to say. It makes something of men—learning. A house that's full of books makes a different kind of people. Oh, of course, if the books aren't there just to show off.

GRANDMOTHER

Like in Mary Baldwin's new house.

SILAS

[*Trying hard to see it.*] It's not the learning itself—it's the life that grows up from learning. Learning's like soil. Like—like fertilizer. Get richer. See more. Feel more. You believe that?

FEJEVARY

Culture should do it.

SILAS

Does in your house. You somehow know how it is for the other fellow more 'n we do.

### GRANDMOTHER

Well, Silas Morton, when you've your wood to chop an' your water to carry, when you kill your own cattle and hogs, tend your own horses and hens, make your butter, soap, and cook for whoever the Lord sends,— there's none too many hours of the day left to be polite in.

### SILAS

You're right, mother. It had to be that way. But now that we buy our soap,—we don't want to say what soap-making made us.

### GRANDMOTHER

We're honest.

### SILAS

Yes. In a way. But there's another kind o' honesty, seems to me, goes with that more seein' kind of kindness. Our honesty with the Indians was little to brag on.

### GRANDMOTHER

You fret more about the Indians than anybody else does.

### SILAS

To look out at that hill sometimes makes me ashamed.

### GRANDMOTHER

Land sakes, you didn't do it. It was the government. And what a government does is nothing for a person to be ashamed of.

### SILAS

I don't know about that. Why is *he* here? Why is Felix Fejevary not rich and grand in Hungary today? 'Cause he was ashamed of what his government was.

### GRANDMOTHER

Well, that was a foreign government.

### SILAS

A seeing how 'tis for the other person—a *bein'* that other person, kind of honesty. Joke of it, 'twould do something for *you*. 'Twould 'a done something for us to have *been* Indians a little more. My father used to talk about Blackhawk—they was friends. I saw Blackhawk once—when I was a boy. [*To* FEJEVARY.] Guess I told you. You know what he looked like? He looked like the great of the earth. Noble. Noble like the forests—and the Mississippi—and the stars. His face was long and thin and you could see the bones and the bones were beautiful. Looked like something that's never been caught. He was something many nights in his canoe had made him. Sometimes I feel that the land itself has got a mind and that the land would rather have had the Indians.

### GRANDMOTHER

Well don't let folks hear you say it. They'd think you was plum crazy.

### SILAS

I s'pose they would. [*Turning to* FEJEVARY.] But after you've walked a long time over the earth—and you all alone, didn't you ever feel something coming up from it that's like thought?

FEJEVARY

I'm afraid I never did. But—I wish I had.

SILAS

I love land—this land. I suppose that's why I never have the feeling that I own it.

GRANDMOTHER

If you don't own it—I want to know! What do you think we come here for—your father and me? What do you think we left our folks for—left the world of white folks—schools and stores and doctors and set out in a covered wagon for we didn't know what? We lost a horse. Lost our way—weeks longer than we thought 'twould be. You were born in that covered wagon. You know that. But what you don't know is what *that's* like—without your own roof—or fire—without—

[*She turns her face away.*]

SILAS

No. No, mother, of course not. Now—now isn't this too bad? I don't say things right. It's because I never went to school.

GRANDMOTHER

[*Her face shielded.*] You went to school two winters.

SILAS

Yes. Yes, mother. So I did. And I'm glad I did.

GRANDMOTHER

[*With the determination of one who will not have her own pain looked at.*] Mrs. Fejevary's pansy bed doing well this summer?

FEJEVARY

It's beautiful this summer. She was so pleased with the new purple kind you gave her. I do wish you could get over and see them.

GRANDMOTHER

Yes. Well, I've seen lots of pansies. Suppose it was pretty fine-sounding speeches they had in town?

FEJEVARY

Too fine sounding to seem much like the war.

SILAS

I'd like to go to a war celebration where they never mentioned war. There'd be a way to celebrate victory. [*Hearing a step, looking out.*] Mother, here's Felix.
[FELIX, *a well-dressed young man comes in.*

GRANDMOTHER

How do, Felix?

FELIX

And how do you do, Grandmother Morton?

GRANDMOTHER

Well, I'm still here.

FELIX

Of course you are. It wouldn't be coming home if you weren't.

### GRANDMOTHER

I've got some cookies for you, Felix. I set 'em out, so you wouldn't have to steal them. John and Felix was hard on the cookie jar.

### FELIX

Where is John?

### SILAS

[*Who is pouring a glass of wine for* FELIX.] You've not seen John yet? He was in town for the exercises. I bet those young devils ran off to the race-track. I heard whisperin' goin' round. But everybody'll be home sometime. Mary and the girls—don't ask me where they are. They'll drive old Bess all over the county before they drive her to the barn. Your father and I come on home 'cause I wanted to have a talk with him.

### FELIX

Getting into the old uniforms makes you want to talk it all over again?

### SILAS

The war? Well, we did do that. But all that makes me want to talk about what's to come, about—what 'twas all for. Great things are to come, Felix. And before you are through.

### FELIX

I've been thinking about them myself—walking around the town today. It's grown so much this year, and in a way that means more growing—that big glocuse plant going up down the river, the new lumber mill—all that means many more people.

### FEJEVARY

And they've even bought ground for a steel works.

### SILAS

Yes, a city will rise from these cornfields—a big rich place—that's bound to be. It's written in the lay o' the land and the way the river flows. But first tell us about Harvard College, Felix. Ain't it a fine thing for us all to have Felix coming home from that wonderful place!

### FELIX

You make it seem wonderful.

### SILAS

Ah, you know it's wonderful—know it so well you don't have to say it. It's something you've got. But to me it's wonderful the way the stars are wonderful—this place where all that the world has learned is to be drawn from like—like a spring.

### FELIX

You almost say what Matthew Arnold says—a distinguished new English writer who speaks of: "The best that has been thought and said in the world."

### SILAS

"The best that has been thought and said in the world!" [*Slowly rising, and as if the dream of years is bringing him to his feet.*] That's what that hill is for! [*Pointing.*] Don't you see it? End of our trail, we climb a hill and plant a college. Plant a college, so's after we are gone that college says for us, says in people learning has made more: "This is why we took this land!"

### GRANDMOTHER

[*Incredulous.*] You mean, Silas, you're going to *give the hill away?*

### SILAS

The hill at the end of our trail—how could we keep that?

### GRANDMOTHER

Well I want to know why not! Hill or level—land's land and not a thing you give away.

### SILAS

Well, don't scold *me*. I'm not giving it away. It's giving itself away, get down to it.

### GRANDMOTHER

Don't talk to me as if I was feeble-minded.

### SILAS

I'm talking with all the mind I've got. If there's not mind in what I say, it's because I've got no mind. But I have got a mind. [*To* FEJEVARY, *humorously.*] Haven't I? You ought to know. Seeing as you gave it to me.

### FEJEVARY

Ah no—I didn't give it to you.

### Silas

Well, you made me know 'twas there. You said things that woke things in me and I thought about them as I ploughed. And that made me know there had to be a college there—wake things in minds—so ploughin's more than ploughing. What do you say, Felix?

### Felix

It—it's a big idea, Uncle Silas. I love the way you put it. It's only that I'm wondering—

### Silas

Wondering how it can ever be a Harvard College? Well it can't. And it needn't be. [*Stubbornly.*] It's a college in the cornfields—where the Indian maize once grew. And it's for the boys of the cornfields—and the girls. There's few can go to Harvard College—but more can climb that hill. [*Turn of the head from the hill to* Felix.] Harvard on a hill? [*As* Felix *smiles no,* Silas *turns back to the hill.*] A college should be on a hill. They can see it then from far around. See it as they go out to the barn in the morning; see it when they're shutting up at night. 'Twill make a difference—even to them that never go.

### Grandmother

Now, Silas—don't be hasty.

### Silas

Hasty? It's been company to me for years. Came to me one night—must 'a' been ten years ago—middle of a starry night as I was comin' home from your place. [*To* Fejevary.] I'd gone over to lend a hand with a sick horse an'—

FEJEVARY

[*With a grateful smile.*] That was nothing new.

SILAS

Well, say, I'd sit up with a sick horse that belonged to the meanest man unhung. But—there were stars that night had never been there before. Leastways I'd not seen 'em. And the hill—Felix, in all your travels east, did you ever see anything more beautiful than that hill?

FELIX

It's like sculpture.

SILAS

Hm. [*The wistfulness with which he speaks of that outside his knowledge.*] I s'pose 'tis. It's the way it rises—somehow—as if it knew it rose from wide and fertile lands. I climbed the hill that night. [*To* FEJEVARY.] You'd been talkin'. As we waited between medicines you told me about your life as a young man. All you'd lived through seemed to —open up to you that night—way things do at times. Guess it was 'cause you thought you was goin' to lose your horse. See, that was Colonel, the sorrel, wasn't it?

FEJEVARY

Yes. Good old Colonel.

SILAS

You'd had a long run o' off luck. Hadn't got things back in shape since the war. But say, you didn't lose him, did you?

FEJEVARY

Thanks to you.

SILAS

Thanks to the medicine I keep in the back kitchen.

FEJEVARY

You encouraged him.

GRANDMOTHER

Silas has a way with all the beasts.

SILAS

We've got the same kind of minds—the beasts and me.

GRANDMOTHER

Silas, I wish you wouldn't talk like that—and with Felix just home from Harvard College.

SILAS

Same kind of minds—except that mine goes on a little farther.

GRANDMOTHER

Well, I'm glad to hear you say that.

SILAS

Well, there we sat—you an' me—middle of a starry night, out beside your barn. And I guess it came over you kind of funny you should be there with me—way off the Mississippi, tryin' to save a sick horse. Seemed to—bring your life to life again. You told me what you studied in that fine old university you loved—in

Vienna,—and why you became a revolutionist. The old dreams took hold o' you and you talked—way you used to, I suppose. The years, o'course, had rubbed some of it off. Your face as you went on about the vision—you called it, vision of what life could be. I knew that night there was things I had never got wind of. When I went away—knew I ought to go home to bed—hayin' at daybreak. "Go to bed?" I said to myself. "Strike this dead when you've never had it before, may never have it again?" I climbed the hill. Blackhawk was there.

### GRANDMOTHER

Why he was *dead*.

### SILAS

He was there—on his own old hill, with me and the stars. And I said to him—

### GRANDMOTHER

Silas!

### SILAS

Says I to him, "Yes—that's true; it's more yours than mine, you had it first and loved it best. But it's neither yours nor mine,—though both yours and mine. Not my hill, not your hill, but—hill of vision, said I to him. Here shall come visions of a better world than was ever seen by you or me, old Indian chief. Oh, I was drunk, plum drunk.

### GRANDMOTHER

I should think you was. And what about the next day's hay?

### SILAS

A day in the hayfield is a day's hayin'—but a night on the hill—

### FELIX

We don't have them often, do we, Uncle Silas?

### SILAS

I wouldn't 'a had that one but for your father, Felix. Thank God they drove you out o' Hungary! And it's all so dog-gone *queer*. Ain't it queer how things blow from mind to mind—like seeds. Lord A'mighty—you don't know where they'll take hold.

[*Children's voices off.*

### GRANDMOTHER

There come those children up from the creek—soppin' wet, I warrant. Well, I don't know how children ever get raised. But we raise more of 'em than we used to. I buried three—first ten years I was here. Needn't 'a happened—if we'd known what we know now, and if we hadn't been alone. [*With all her strength.*] I don't know what you mean—the hill's not yours!

### SILAS

It's the future's, mother—so's we can know more than we know now.

### GRANDMOTHER

We know it now. 'Twas then we didn't know it. I worked for that hill! And I tell you to leave it to your own children.

SILAS

There's other land for my own children. This is for all the children.

GRANDMOTHER

What's all the children to you?

SILAS

[*Derisively.*] Oh, mother—what a thing for you to say! You who were never too tired to give up your own bed so the stranger could have a better bed.

GRANDMOTHER

That was different. They was folks on their way.

FEJEVARY

So are we.

[SILAS *turns to him with quick appreciation.*

GRANDMOTHER

That's just talk. We're settled now. Children of other old settlers are getting rich. I should think you'd want yours to.

SILAS

I want other things more. I want to pay my debts 'fore I'm too old to know they're debts.

GRANDMOTHER

[*Momentarily startled.*] Debts? Huh! More talk. You don't owe any man.

SILAS

I owe him. [*Nodding to* FEJEVARY.] And the red boys here before me.

GRANDMOTHER

Fiddlesticks.

FELIX

You haven't read Darwin, have you, Uncle Silas?

SILAS

Who?

FELIX

Darwin, the great new man—and his theory of the survival of the fittest?

SILAS

No. No, I don't know things like that, Felix.

FELIX

I think he might make you feel better about the Indians. In the struggle for existence, many must go down. The fittest survive. This—had to be.

SILAS

Us and the Indians? Guess I don't know what you mean—fittest.

FELIX

He calls it that. Best fitted to the place in which one finds one's self, having the qualities that can best cope with conditions—do things. From the beginning of life it's been like that. He shows the growth of life

from forms that were barely alive, the lowest animal
forms—jellyfish—up to man.

#### SILAS

Oh, yes, that's the thing the churches are so upset
about—that we come from monkeys.

#### FELIX

Yes. One family of ape is the direct ancestor of man.

#### GRANDMOTHER

You'd better read your Bible, Felix.

#### SILAS

Do people believe this?

#### FELIX

The whole intellectual world is at war about it. The
best scientists accept it. Teachers are losing their posi-
tions for believing it. Of course, ministers can't believe it.

#### GRANDMOTHER

I should think not. Anyway, what's the use believing
a thing that's so discouraging?

#### FEJEVARY

[*Gently.*] But is it that? It almost seems to me we
have to accept it because it is so encouraging. [*Holding
out his hand.*] Why have we hands?

#### GRANDMOTHER

Cause God gave them to us, I s'pose.

#### Fejevary

But that's rather general, and there isn't much in it to give us self-confidence. But when you think we have hands because ages back—before life had taken form as man, there was an impulse to do what had never been done—when you think that we have hands today because from the first of life there have been adventurers —those of best brain and courage who wanted to be more than life had been, and that from aspiration has come doing, and doing has shaped the thing with which to do—it gives our hand a history which should make us want to use it well.

#### Silas

[*Breathed from deep.*] Well, by God! And you've known this all this while! Dog-gone you—why didn't you tell me?

#### Fejevary

I've been thinking about it. I haven't known what to believe. This hurts—beliefs of earlier years.

#### Felix

The things it hurts will have to go.

#### Fejevary

I don't know about that, Felix. Perhaps in time we'll find truth in them.

#### Felix

Oh, if you feel that way, father.

#### Fejevary

Don't be kind to me, my boy, I'm not that old.

### Silas

But think what it is you've said! If it's true that we *made* ourselves—made ourselves out of the wanting to be more—created ourselves you might say, by our own courage—our—what is it?—aspiration. Why, I can't take it in. I haven't got the mind to take it in. And what mind I have got says no. It's too—

### Fejevary

It fights with what's there.

### Silas

[*Nodding.*] But it's like I got this [*very slowly*] other way around. From underneath. As if I'd known it all along—but have just found out I know it! Yes. The earth told me. The beasts told me.

### Grandmother

Fine place to learn things from.

### Silas

Anyhow, haven't I seen it? [*To* Fejevary.] In your face haven't I seen thinking make a finer face? How long has this taken Felix to—well, you might say, bring us where we are now?

### Felix

Oh, we don't know how many millions of years since earth first stirred.

### Silas

Then we are what we are because through all that time there've been them that wanted to be more than life had been.

FELIX

That's it, Uncle Silas.

SILAS

But—why, then we aren't *finished* yet!

FEJEVARY

No. We take it on from here.

SILAS

[*Slowly.*] Then if we don't be—the most we can be,
if we don't be more than life has been, we go back on
all that life behind us ; go back on—the—
[*Unable to formulate it, he looks to*
FEJEVARY.

FEJEVARY

Go back on the dreaming and the daring of a million
years.
[*After a moment's pause* SILAS *gets up,
opens the closet door.*

GRANDMOTHER

Silas, what you doing?

SILAS

[*Who has taken out a box.*] I'm lookin' for the
deed to the hill.

GRANDMOTHER

What you going to do with it?

SILAS

I'm goin' to get it out of my hands.

### GRANDMOTHER

Get it out of your hands? [*He has it now.*] Deed your father got from the government the very year the government got it from the Indians? [*Rising.*] Give me that! [*She turns to* FEJEVARY.] Tell him he's crazy. We got the best land 'cause we was first here. We got a right to keep it.

### FEJEVARY

[*Going soothingly to her.*] It's true, Silas, it is a serious thing to give away one's land.

### SILAS

You ought to know. You did it. Are you sorry you did it?

### FEJEVARY

No. But wasn't that different?

### SILAS

How was it different? Yours was a fight to make life more, wasn't it? Well, let this be our way.

### GRANDMOTHER

What's all that got to do with giving up the land that should provide for your own children?

### SILAS

Isn't it providing for them to give them a better world to live in? Felix—you're young, I ask you, ain't it providing for them to give them a chance to be more than we are?

### FELIX

I think you're entirely right, Uncle Silas. But it's the practical question that—

### SILAS

If you're right, the practical question is just a thing to fix up.

### FEJEVARY

I fear you don't realize the immense amount of money required to finance a college. The land would be a start. You would have to interest rich men; you'd have to have a community in sympathy with the thing you wanted to do.

### GRANDMOTHER

Can't you see, Silas, that we're all against you?

### SILAS

All against me? [*To* FEJEVARY.] But how can you be? Look at the land we walked in and took! Was there ever such a chance to make life more? Why the buffalo here before us was more than we if we do nothing but prosper! God damn us if we sit here rich and fat and forget man's in the makin'. [*Affirming against this.*] There will one day be a college in these cornfields by the Mississippi because long ago a great dream was fought for in Hungary. And I say to that old dream, Wake up, old dream! Wake up and fight! You say rich men. [*Holding it out, but it is not taken.*]

I give you this deed to take to rich men to show them one man believes enough in this to give the best land he's got. That ought to make rich men stop and think.

#### GRANDMOTHER

Stop and think he's a fool.

#### SILAS

[*To* FEJEVARY.]  It's you can make them know he's not a fool.  When you tell this way you can tell it, they'll feel in you what's more than them.  They'll listen.

#### GRANDMOTHER

I tell you, Silas, folks are too busy.

#### SILAS

"Too busy!"  Too busy bein' nothin'?  If it's true that we created ourselves out of the thoughts that came, then thought is not something *outside* the business of life.  Thought—[*with his gift for wonder*] why thought's our *chance*.  I know now.  Why I can't forget the Indians.  We killed their joy before we killed them.  We made them less.  [*To* FEJEVARY, *and as if sure he is now making it clear.*]  I got to give it back—their hill.  I give it back to joy—a better joy—joy o' aspiration.

#### FEJEVARY

[*Moved but unconvinced.*]  But, my friend, there are men who have no aspiration.  That's why, to me, this is as a light shining from too far.

#### GRANDMOTHER

[*Old things waked in her.*]  Light shining from far.  We used to do that.  We never pulled the curtains.  I used to want to—you like to be to yourself when night comes—but we always left a lighted window for the traveler who'd lost his way.

FELIX

I should think that would have exposed you to the Indians.

GRANDMOTHER

Yes. [*Impatiently.*] Well, you can't put out a light just because it may light the wrong person.

FEJEVARY

No. [*And this is as a light to him. He turns to the hill.*] No.

SILAS

[*With gentleness, and profoundly.*] That's it. Look again. Maybe your eyes are stronger now. Don't you see it? I see that college rising as from the soil itself, as if it was what come at the last of that thinking that breathes from the earth. I see it—but I want to know it's real before I stop knowing. Then maybe I can lie under the same sod with the red boys and not be ashamed. We're not old! Let's fight! Wake in other men what you woke in me!

FEJEVARY

And so could I pay my debt to America.

[*His hand goes out.*

SILAS

[*Giving him the deed.*] And to the dreams of a million years!

[*Standing near the open door their hands
are gripped in compact.*

(CURTAIN)

# ACT TWO

SCENE: *A corridor in the library of Morton College, October of the year 1920, upon the occasion of the fortieth anniversary of its founding. This is an open place in the stacks of books, which are seen at both sides. There is a reading table before the big rear window. This window opens out, but does not extend to the floor; only a part of its height is seen, indicating a very high window. Outside is seen the top of a tree.*

*This outer wall of the building is on a slant, so that the entrance right is rear, and the left is front. Right front is a section of a huge square column. On the rear of this, facing the window, is hung a picture of* SILAS MORTON. *Two men are standing before this portrait.*

SENATOR LEWIS *is the middle-western state senator. He is not of the city from which Morton College rises, but of a more country community farther in-state.* FELIX FEJEVARY, *now nearing the age of his father in the first act, is an American of the more sophisticated type—prosperous, having the poise of success in affairs and place in society.*

### SENATOR

And this was the boy who founded the place, eh? It was his idea?

FEJEVARY

Yes, and his hill. I was there the afternoon he told my father there must be a college here. I wasn't any older then than my boy is now.

[*As if himself surprised by this.*

SENATOR

Well, he enlisted a good man when he let you in on it. I've been told the college wouldn't be what it is today but for you, Mr. Fejevary.

FEJEVARY

I have a sentiment about it, and where our sentiment is, there our work goes also.

SENATOR

Yes. Well, it was those mainsprings of sentiment that won the war.

[*He is pleased with this.*

FEJEVARY

[*Nodding.*] Morton College did her part in winning the war.

SENATOR

I know. A fine showing.

FEJEVARY

And we're holding up our end right along. You'll see the boys drill this afternoon. It's a great place for them, here on the hill—shows up from so far around. They're a fine lot of fellows. You know, I presume, that they went in as strike-breakers during the trouble down here at the steel works. The plant would have

had to close but for Morton College.   That's one reason
I venture to propose this thing of a state appropriation
for enlargement.   Why don't we sit down a moment?
There's no conflict with the state university—they have
their territory, we have ours.   Ours is an important one
—industrially speaking.   The state will lose nothing in
having a good strong college here—a one-hundred-per-
cent-American college.

SENATOR

I admit I am very favorably impressed.

FEJEVARY

I hope you'll tell your committee so—and let me
have a chance to talk to them.

SENATOR

Let's see, haven't you a pretty radical man here?

FEJEVARY

I wonder if you mean Holden?

SENATOR

Holden's the man.   I've read things that make me
question his Americanism.

FEJEVARY

Oh—[*Gesture of depreciation.*]   I don't think he is
so much a radical as a particularly human human-
being.

SENATOR

But we don't want radical human beings.

FEJEVARY

He has a genuine sympathy with youth. That's invaluable in a teacher, you know. And then—he's a scholar.

> [*He betrays here his feeling of superiority to his companion, but too subtly for his companion to get it.*

SENATOR

Oh—scholar. We can get scholars enough. What we want is Americans.

FEJEVARY

Americans who are scholars.

SENATOR

You can pick 'em off every bush—pay them a little more than they're paid in some other cheap John College. Excuse me—I don't mean this is a cheap John College.

FEJEVARY

Of course not. One couldn't think that of Morton College. But that—pay them a little more, interests me. That's another reason I want to talk to your committee on appropriations. We claim to value education and then we let highly trained, gifted men fall behind the plumber.

SENATOR

Well, that's the plumber's fault. Let the teachers talk to the plumber.

### Fejevary

[*With a smile.*] No. Better not let them talk to the plumber. He might tell them what to do about it, In fact, is telling them.

### Senator

That's ridiculous. They can't serve both God and mammon.

### Fejevary

Then let God give them mammon. I mean, let the state appropriate.

### Senator

Of course this state, Mr. Fejevary, appropriates no money for radicals. Excuse me, but why do you keep this man Holden?

### Fejevary

In the scholar's world we're known because of him. And really, Holden's not a radical—in the worst sense. What he doesn't see is—expediency. Not enough the man of affairs to realize that we can't always have literally what we have theoretically. He's an idealist. Something of the—man of vision.

### Senator

If he had the right vision he'd see that we don't every minute have literally what we have theoretically because we're fighting to keep the thing we have. Oh, I sometimes think the man of affairs has the only vision. Take you, Mr. Fejevary—a banker. These teachers— books—books! [*Pushing all books back.*] Why, if they had to take for one day the responsibility that falls on your shoulders—big decisions to make—man among men—and all the time worries, irritations, particularly now with labor riding the high horse like a fool! I know something about these things. I went to the State House because my community persuaded me it was my duty. But I'm the man of affairs, myself.

#### FEJEVARY

Oh yes, I know. Your company did much to develop that whole northern part of the state.

#### SENATOR

I think I may say we did. Well, that's why, after three sessions, I'm chairman of the appropriations committee. I know how to use money to promote the state. So—teacher? That would be a perpetual vacation to me. Now, if you want my advice, Mr. Fejevary,—I think your case before the state would be stronger if you let this fellow Holden go.

#### FEJEVARY

I'm going to have a talk with Professor Holden.

#### SENATOR

Tell him it's for his own good. The idea of a college professor standing up for conscientious objectors!

#### FEJEVARY

That doesn't quite state the case. Fred Jordan was one of Holden's students—a student he valued. He felt Jordan was perfectly sincere in his objection.

SENATOR

Sincere in his objections! The nerve of him thinking it was his business to be sincere!

FEJEVARY

He was expelled from college—you may remember; that was how we felt about it.

SENATOR

I should hope so.

FEJEVARY

Holden fought that, but within the college. What brought him into the papers was his protest against the way the boy has been treated in prison.

SENATOR

What's the difference how he's treated? You know how I'd treat him? [*A movement as though pulling a trigger.*] If I didn't know you for the American you are, I wouldn't understand your speaking so calmly.

FEJEVARY

I'm simply trying to see it all sides around.

SENATOR

Makes me see red.

FEJEVARY

[*With a smile.*] But we mustn't meet red with red.

SENATOR

What's Holden fussing about—that they don't give him caviar on toast?

FEJEVARY

That they didn't give him books. Holden felt it was his business to fuss about that.

SENATOR

Well, when your own boy 'stead of whining around about his conscience, stood up and offered his life!

FEJEVARY

Yes. And my nephew gave his life.

SENATOR

That so?

FEJEVARY

Silas Morton's grandson died in France. My sister Madeline married Ira Morton, son of Silas Morton.

SENATOR

I knew there was a family connection between you and the Mortons.

FEJEVARY

[*Speaking with reserve.*] They played together as children and married as soon as they were grown up.

SENATOR

So this was your sister's boy? [FEJEVARY *nods.*] One of the mothers to give her son!

FEJEVARY

[*Speaking of her with effort.*] My sister died— long ago. [*Pulled to an old feeling; with an effort releasing himself.*] But Ira is still out at the old place—

place the Morton's took up when they reached the end of their trail—as Uncle Silas used to put it. Why, it's a hundred years ago that Grandmother Morton began—making cookies here. She was the first white woman in this county.

#### SENATOR

Proud woman! To have begun the life of this state! Oh, our pioneers! If they could only see us now, and know what they did! [FEJEVARY *is silent; he does not look quite happy.*] I suppose Silas Morton's son is active in the college management.

#### FEJEVARY

No, Ira is not a social being. Fred's death about finished him He had been—strange for years, ever since my sister died—when the children were little. It was—[*again pulled back to that old feeling*] under pretty terrible circumstances.

#### SENATOR

I can see that you thought a great deal of your sister, Mr. Fejevary.

#### FEJEVARY

Oh, she was beautiful and—[*bitterly*] it shouldn't have gone like that.

#### SENATOR

Seems to me I've heard something about Silas Morton's son— though perhaps it wasn't this one.

#### FEJEVARY

Ira is the only one living here now; the others have gone farther west.

SENATOR

Isn't there something about corn?

FEJEVARY

Yes. His corn has several years taken the prize—
best in the state. He's experimented with it—created
a new kind. They've given it his name—Morton corn.
It seems corn is rather fascinating to work with—very
mutable stuff. It's a good thing Ira has it, for it's
about the only thing he does care for now. Oh, Madeline, of course. He has a daughter here in the college—
Madeline Morton, senior this year—one of our best
students. I'd like to have you meet Madeline—she's
a great girl, though—peculiar.

SENATOR

Well, that makes a girl interesting, if she isn't peculiar the wrong way. Sounds as if her home life might
make her a little peculiar.

FEJEVARY

Madeline stays here in town with us a good part of
the time. Mrs. Fejevary is devoted to her—we all are.
[*A boy starts to come through from right.*] Hello,
see who's here. This is my boy. Horace, this is
Senator Lewis, who is interested in the college.

HORACE

[*Shaking hands.*] How do you do, Senator Lewis?

SENATOR

Pleased to see you, my boy.

HORACE

Am I butting in?

FEJEVARY

Not seriously; but what are you doing in the library? I thought this was a day off.

HORACE

I'm looking for a book.

FEJEVARY

[*Affectionately bantering.*] You are, Horace? Now how does that happen?

HORACE

I want the speeches of Abraham Lincoln.

SENATOR

You couldn't do better.

HORACE

I'll show those dirty dagoes where they get off!

FEJEVARY

You couldn't show them a little more elegantly?

HORACE

I'm going to sick the Legion on 'em.

FEJEVARY

Are you talking about the Hindus?

HORACE

Yes, the dirty dagoes.

FEJEVARY

Hindus aren't dagoes you know, Horace.

HORACE

Well, what's the difference? This foreign element gets my goat.

SENATOR

My boy, you talk like an American. But what do you mean—Hindus?

FEJEVARY

There are two young Hindus here as students. And they're good students.

HORACE

Sissies.

FEJEVARY

But they must preach the gospel of free India—non-British India.

SENATOR

Oh, that won't do.

HORACE

They're nothing but Reds, I'll say. Well, one of 'em's going back to get his.

[*Grins.*

FEJEVARY

There were three of them last year. One of them is wanted back home.

SENATOR

I remember now.   He's to be deported.

HORACE

And when they get him—[*Movement as of pulling a rope.*]   They hang there.

FEJEVARY

The other two protest against our not fighting the deportation of their comrade.   They insist it means death to him.   [*Brushing off a thing that is inclined to worry him.*]   But we can't handle India's affairs.

SENATOR

I should think not!

HORACE

Why, England's our ally!   That's what I told them. But you can't argue with people like that.   Just wait till I find the speeches of Abraham Lincoln!

[*Passes through to left.*

SENATOR

Fine boy you have, Mr. Fejevary.

FEJEVARY

He's a live one.   You should see him in a football game.   Wouldn't hurt my feelings in the least to have him a little more of a student, but—

SENATOR

Oh, well, you want him to be a regular fellow, don't you, and grow into a man among men?

FEJEVARY

He'll do that, I think. It was he who organized our
boys for the steel strike—went right in himself and
took a striker's job. He came home with a black eye
one night, presented to him by a picket who started
something by calling him a scab. But Horace wasn't
thinking about his eye. According to him, it was not in
the class with the striker's upper lip. "Father," he
said, "I gave him more red than he could swallow. The
blood just—" Well, I'll spare you—but Horace's
muscle is one hundred per cent American. [*Going to
the window.*] Let me show you something. You can
see the old Morton place off on that first little hill.
[*Pointing left.*] The first rise beyond the valley.

SENATOR

The long low house?

FEJEVARY

That's it. You see the town for the most part swung
around the other side of the hill, so the Morton place
is still a farm.

SENATOR

But you're growing all the while. The town'll take
the cornfield yet.

FEJEVARY

Yes, our steel works is making us a city.

SENATOR

And this old boy [*turning to the portrait of* SILAS
MORTON] can look out on his old home—and watch the
valley grow.

#### Fejevary

Yes—that was my idea. His picture really should be in Memorial Hall, but I thought Uncle Silas would like to be up here among the books, and facing the old place. [*With a laugh.*] I confess to being a little sentimental.

#### Senator

We Americans have lots of sentiment, Mr. Fejevary. It's what makes us—what we are. [Fejevary *does not speak; there are times when the senator seems to trouble him.*] Well, this is a great site for a college. You can see it from the whole country round.

#### Fejevary

Yes, that was Uncle Silas' idea. He had a reverence for education. It grew, in part, out of his feeling for my father. He was a poet—really, Uncle Silas. [*Looking at the picture.*] He gave this hill for a college that we might become a deeper, more sensitive people—

> [*Two girls, convulsed with the giggles, come tumbling in.*

#### Doris

[*Confused.*] Oh—oh, excuse us.

#### Fussie

[*Foolishly.*] We didn't know anybody was here.
> [Mr. Fejevary *looks at them sternly. The girls retreat.*

#### Senator

[*Laughing.*] Oh, well, girls will be girls. I've got three of my own.
> [*Horace come back, carrying an open book.*

#### Horace

Say, this must be a misprint.

#### Fejevary

[*Glancing at the back of the book.*]   Oh, I think
not.

#### Horace

From his first inaugural address to Congress,
March 4, 1861. [*Reads.*] "This country with its
institutions belongs to the people who inhabit it."
Well, that's all right. "Whenever they shall grow
weary of the existing government, they can exercise
their constitutional right of amending it,"—[*after
a brief consideration*] I suppose that that's all right—
but listen! "or their *revolutionary* right to dismember
or overthrow it."

#### Fejevary

He was speaking in another age.   An age of different
values.

#### Senator

Terms change their significance from generation to
generation.

#### Horace

I suppose they do—but that puts me in bad with these
lice.   They quoted this and I said they were liars.

#### Senator

And what's the idea?   They're weary of our existing
government and are about to dismember or overthrow
it?

HORACE

I guess that's the dope.

FEJEVARY

Look here, Horace—speak accurately. Was it in relation to America they quoted this?

HORACE

Well, maybe they were talking about India then. But they were standing up for being revolutionists. We were giving them an earful about it, and then they sprung Lincoln on us. Got their nerve—I'll say—quoting Lincoln to us.

SENATOR

The fact that they are quoting it shows it's being misapplied.

HORACE

[*Approvingly.*] I'll tell them that. But gee—Lincoln oughta been more careful what he said. Ignorant people don't know how to take such things.

[*Goes back with book.*

FEJEVARY

Want to take a look through the rest of the library? We haven't been up this way yet—[*Motioning left.*] We need a better scientific library. [*They are leaving now.*] Oh, we simply must have more money. The whole thing is fairly bursting its shell.

DORIS

[*Venturing in cautiously, from the other side, looking back, beckoning.*] They've gone.

FUSSIE

Sure?

DORIS

Well, are they here? And I saw them, I tell you—
they went up to science.

FUSSIE

[*Moving the* SENATOR'S *hat on the table.*]   But
they'll come back.

DORIS

What if they do? We're only looking at a book.
[*Running her hand along the books*]   Matthew Arnold.
[*Takes a paper from* FUSSIE, *puts it in
the book. They are bent with gig-
gling as Horace returns.*

HORACE

For the love o' Pete, what's the joke? [*Taking the
book from the helpless girl.*]   Matthew Arnold.   My
idea of nowhere to go for a laugh. When I wrote my
theme on him last week he was so dry I had to go out
and get a Morton Sundee. [*The girls are freshly at-
tacked, though all of this in a subdued way, mindful of
others in the library.*]   Say, how'd you get that way?

DORIS

Now, Horace, don't you *tell*.

HORACE

What'd I tell. except—[*seeing the paper*]   Um hum
—what's this?

#### DORIS

[*Trying to get it from him.*] Horace, now *don't* you.
[*A tussle.*] You great strong mean thing! Fussie!
Make him *stop*.

[*She gets the paper by tearing it.*

#### HORACE

My dad's around here—showing the college off to a
politician. If you don't come across with that sheet of
mystery, I'll back you both out there [*starts to do it*]
and—

#### DORIS

Horace! You're just *horrid*.

#### HORACE

Sure I'm horrid. That's the way I want to be.
[*Takes the paper, reads.*] "To Eben
      You are the idol of my dreams
      I worship from afar."
What *is* this?

#### FUSSIE

Now, listen, Horace, and don't you *tell*. You know
Eben Weeks. He's the homeliest man in school.
Wouldn't you say so?

#### HORACE

Awful jay. Like to get some of the jays out of here.

#### DORIS

But listen. Of course, no girl would *look* at him.
So we've thought up the most *killing* joke. [*Stopped
by giggles from herself and* FUSSIE.] Now, he hasn't

handed in his Matthew Arnold dope. I heard old Mac hold him up for it—and what'd you think he said? That he'd been *ploughing*. Said he was trying to run a farm and go to college at the same time! Isn't it a *scream?*

HORACE

We oughta—make it more unpleasant for some of those jays. Gives the school a bad name.

FUSSIE

But, listen, Horace, honest—you'll just *die*. He said he was going to get the book this afternoon. Now you know what he *looks* like, but he turns to—
[*Both girls are convulsed.*

DORIS

It'll get him all fussed up! And for nothing at all!

HORACE

Too bad that class of people come here. I think I'll go to Harvard next year. Haven't broken it to my parental—but I've about made up my mind.

DORIS

Don't you think Morton's a good school, Horace?

HORACE

Morton's all right. Fine for the—[*kindly*] people who would naturally come here. But one gets an acquaintance at Harvard. Where'd'y' want these passionate lines?
[FUSSIE *and* DORIS *are off again convulsed.*

#### HORACE

[*Eye falling on the page where he opens the book.*] Say, old Bones could spill the English—what? Listen to this flyer: "For when we say that culture is to know the best that has been thought and said in the world, we simply imply that for culture a system directly tending to that end is necessary in our reading." [*He reads it with mock solemnity, delighting* FUSSIE *and* DORIS.] "The best that has been thought and said in the world!"

[MADELINE MORTON *comes in from right; she carries a tennis racket.*

#### MADELINE

[*Both critical and good-humored.*] You haven't made a large contribution to that, have you, Horace?

#### HORACE

Madeline, you don't want to let this sarcastic habit grow on you.

#### MADELINE

Thanks for the tip.

#### FUSSIE

Oh—*Madeline.* [*Holds out her hand to take the book from* HORACE *and show it to* MADELINE.] You know—

#### DORIS

S—h. Don't be silly. [*To cover this*] Who you playing with?

#### HORACE

Want me to play with you, Madeline?

MADELINE

[*Genially.*] I'd rather play with you than talk to you.

HORACE

Same here.

FUSSIE

Aren't cousins affectionate?

MADELINE

[*Moving through to the other part of the library.*] But first I'm looking for a book.

HORACE

Well, I can tell you without your looking it up, he did say it. But that was an age of different values. Anyway, the fact that they're quoting it shows it's being misapplied.

MADELINE

[*Smiling.*] Father said so.

HORACE

[*On his dignity.*] Oh, of course—if you don't want to be serious.

[MADELINE *laughs and passes on through.*

DORIS

What are you two talking about?

HORACE

Madeline happened to overhear a little discussion down on the campus.

FUSSIE

Listen. You know something? Sometimes I think Madeline Morton is a highbrow in disguise.

HORACE

Say, you don't want to start anything like that. Madeline's all right. She and I treat each other rough —but that's being in the family.

FUSSIE

Well, I'll *tell* you something. I heard Professor Holden say Madeline Morton had a great deal more mind than she'd let herself know.

HORACE

Oh, well—Holden, he's erratic. Look at how popular Madeline is.

DORIS

I should *say*. What's the matter with you, Fussie?

FUSSIE

Oh, I didn't mean it really *hurt* her.

HORACE

Guess it don't hurt her much at a dance. Say, what's this new jazz they were springing last night?

DORIS

I know! Now look here, Horace—L'me show you.
[*She shows him a step.*

HORACE

I get you.

[*He begins to dance with her; the book
he holds slips to the floor. He kicks
it under the table.*

FUSSIE

Be *careful*. They'll be coming back here.

[*Glances off left.*

DORIS

Keep an eye out, Fussie.

FUSSIE

[*From her post.*] They're coming! I tell you, they're *coming!*

DORIS

Horace, come *on*.

[*He teasingly keeps hold of her, continuing the dance. At sound of voices, they run off, right.* FUSSIE *considers rescuing the book, decides she has not time.*

SENATOR

[*At first speaking off.*] Yes, it could be done. There is that surplus, and as long as Morton College is socially valuable—right here above the steel works, and making this feature of military training—[*He has picked up his hat.*] But your Americanism must be unimpeachable, Mr. Fejevary. This man Holden stands in the way.

FEJEVARY

I'm going to have a talk with Professor Holden this afternoon. If he remains he will—[*It is not easy for him to say*] give no trouble. [MADELINE *returns.*] Oh, here's Madeline—Silas Morton's granddaughter, Madeline Fejevary Morton. This is Senator Lewis, Madeline.

SENATOR

[*Holding out his hand.*] How do you do, Miss Morton. I suppose this is a great day for you.

MADELINE

Why—I don't know.

SENATOR

The fortieth anniversary of the founding of your grandfather's college? You must be very proud of your illustrious ancestor.

MADELINE

I get a bit bored with him.

SENATOR

Bored with him? My dear young lady!

MADELINE

I suppose because I've heard so many speeches about him—"The sainted pioneer"—"The grand old man of the prairies"—I'm sure I haven't any idea what he really was like.

FEJEVARY

I've tried to tell you, Madeline.

MADELINE

Yes.

SENATOR

I should think you would be proud to be the grand-daughter of this man of vision.

MADELINE

[*Her smile flashing.*] Wouldn't you hate to be the granddaughter of a phrase?

FEJEVARY

[*Trying to laugh it off.*] Madeline! How absurd.

MADELINE

Well, I'm off for tennis.

[*Nods good-bye and passes on.*

FEJEVARY

[*Calling to her.*] Oh, Madeline, if your Aunt Isabel is out there—will you tell her where we are?

MADELINE

[*Calling back.*] All right.

FEJEVARY

[*After a look at his companion.*] Queer girl, Madeline. Rather—moody.

SENATOR

[*Disapprovingly.*] Well—yes.

FEJEVARY

[*Again trying to laugh it off.*] She's been hearing a great many speeches about her grandfather.

SENATOR

She should be proud to hear them.

FEJEVARY

Of course she should. [*Looking in the direction* MADELINE *has gone.*] I want you to meet my wife, Senator Lewis.

#### SENATOR

I should be pleased to meet Mrs. Fejevary. I have heard what she means to the college—socially.

#### FEJEVARY

I think she has given it something it wouldn't have had without her. Certainly a place in the town that is— good for it. And you haven't met our president yet.

#### SENATOR

Guess I've met the real president.

#### FEJEVARY

Oh—no. I'm merely president of the board of trustees.

#### SENATOR

"Merely!"

#### FEJEVARY

I want you to know President Welling. He's very much the cultivated gentleman.

#### SENATOR

Cultivated gentlemen are all right. I'd hate to see a world they ran.

#### FEJEVARY

[*With a laugh.*] I'll just take a look up here, then we can go down the shorter way.

> [*He goes out right.* SENATOR LEWIS *turns and examines the books.* FUSSIE *slips in, looks at him, hesitates, and then stoops under the table*

*for the Matthew Arnold (and her poem) which* HORACE *has kicked there. He turns.*

FUSSIE

[*Not out from under the table.*] Oh, I was just looking for a book.

SENATOR

Quite a place to look for a book.

FUSSIE

[*Crawling out.*] Yes, it got there. I though I'd put it back. Somebody—might want it.

SENATOR

I see, young lady, that you have a regard for books.

FUSSIE

Oh, yes, I do have a regard for them.

SENATOR

[*Holding out his hand.*] And what is your book?

FUSSIE

Oh—it's—it's nothing.
            [*As he continues to hold out his hand, she reluctantly gives the book.*

SENATOR

[*Solemnly.*] Matthew Arnold? Nothing?

FUSSIE

Oh, I didn't mean *him*.

SENATOR

A master of English! I am glad, young woman, that you value this book.

FUSSIE

Oh yes, I'm—awfully fond of it.
> [*Growing more and more nervous as in turning the pages, he nears the poem.*

SENATOR

I am interested in you young people of Morton College.

FUSSIE

That's so good of you.

SENATOR

What is your favorite study?

FUSSIE

Well—[*An inspiration.*] I like all of them.

SENATOR

Morton College is coming on very fast, I understand.

FUSSIE

Oh, yes, it's getting more and more of the right people. It used to be a little jay, you know. Of course, the Fejevarys give it class. Mrs. Fejevary—isn't she wonderful?

SENATOR

I haven't seen her yet. Waiting here now to meet her.

#### FUSSIE

[*Worried by this.*]   Oh, I must—must be going. Shall I put the book back?

[*Holding out her hand.*

#### SENATOR

No, I'll just look it over a bit.

[*Sits down.*

#### FUSSIE

[*Unable to think of any way of getting it.*]   This is where it belongs.

#### SENATOR

Thank you.

[*Reluctantly she goes out.* SENATOR LEWIS *pursues Matthew Arnold with the conscious air of a half literate man reading a "great book." The* FEJEVARYS *come in.*

#### FEJEVARY

I found my wife, Senator Lewis.

#### AUNT ISABEL

[*She is a woman of social distinction and charm.*] How do you do, Senator Lewis?

[*They shake hands.*

#### SENATOR

It's a great pleasure to meet you, Mrs. Fejevary.

#### AUNT ISABEL

Why don't we carry Senator Lewis home for lunch?

SENATOR

Why, you're very kind.

AUNT ISABEL

I'm sure there's a great deal to talk about, so why not talk comfortably, and really get acquainted? And we want to tell you the whole story of Morton College— the good old American spirit behind it.

SENATOR

I am glad to find you an American, Mrs. Fejevary.

AUNT ISABEL

Oh, we are that. Morton College is one hundred per cent American. Our boys—

[*Her boy* HORACE *rushes in.*

HORACE

[*Wildly.*] Father! Will you go after Madeline? The police have got her!

FEJEVARY

*What!*

AUNT ISABEL

[*As he is getting his breath.*] What absurd thing are you saying, Horace?

HORACE

Awful row down on the campus. The Hindus. I told them to keep their mouths shut about Abraham Lincoln. I told them the fact they were quoting him—

FEJEVARY

Never mind what you told them! What happened?

HORACE

We started to—rustle them along a bit. Why they had *handbills* [*holding one up as if presenting incriminating evidence—the* SENATOR *takes it from him*] telling America what to do about deportation! Not on this campus—I say. So we were—we were putting a stop to it. They resisted—particularly the fat one. The cop at the corner saw the row—came up. He took hold of Bakhshish and when the dirty anarchist didn't move along fast enough, he took hold of him—well, a bit rough, you might say, when up rushes Madeline and calls to the cop, "Let that boy alone!" Gee—I don't know just what did happen—awful mix-up. Next thing I knew Madeline hauled off and pasted the policeman a fierce one with her tennis racket!

SENATOR

She *struck* the officer?

HORACE

I should say she did. Twice. The second time—

AUNT ISABEL

*Horace.* [*Looking at her husband.*] I—I can't believe it.

HORACE

I could have squared it, even then, but for Madeline herself. I told the policeman that she didn't understand—that I was her cousin and apologized for her. And she called over at me, "Better apologize for

yourself!" As if there was any sense to that—and she
—she looked like a *tiger*. Honest, everybody was
afraid of her. I kept right on trying to square it, told
the cop she was the granddaughter of the man that
founded the college—that you were her uncle—he
would have gone off with just the Hindu, fixed this up
later, but Madeline balled it up again—didn't care who
was her uncle—Gee! [*He throws open the window.*]
There! You can see them, at the foot of the hill. A
*nice* thing—member of our family led off to the police
station!

### Fejevary

[*To the* Senator.] Will you excuse me?

### Aunt Isabel

[*Trying to return to the manner of pleasant social
things.*] Senator Lewis will go on home with me, and
you—[*he is hurrying out*] come when you can. [*To
the senator.*] Madeline is such a high-spirited girl.

### Senator

If she had no regard for the living, she might—on
this day of all others—have considered her grandfather's memory.
[*Raises his eyes to the picture of* Silas
Morton.

### Horace

Gee! Wouldn't you *say* so?

(Curtain)

# ACT II

## Scene II

Scene: *The same as Scene I, three hours later. PROFESSOR HOLDEN is seated at the table, books before him. He is a man in the fifties. At the moment his care-worn face is lighted by that lift of the spirit which sometimes rewards the scholar who has imaginative feeling.* HARRY, *a student clerk, comes hurrying in. Looks back.*

HARRY

Here's Professor Holden, Mr. Fejevary.

HOLDEN

Mr. Fejevary is looking for me?

HARRY

Yes.

> [*He goes back, a moment later* MR. FEJEVARY *enters. He has his hat, gloves, stick; seems tired and disturbed.*

HOLDEN

Was I mistaken? I thought our appointment was for five.

FEJEVARY

Quite right. But things have changed, so I wondered if I might have a little talk with you now.

78

HOLDEN

To be sure. [*Rising.*] Shall we go downstairs?

FEJEVARY

I don't know. Nice and quiet up here. [*To* HARRY, *who is now passing through.*] Harry, the library is closed now, is it?

HARRY

Yes, it's locked.

FEJEVARY

And there's no one in here?

HARRY

No, I've been all through.

FEJEVARY

There's a committee downstairs. Oh, this is a terrible day. [*Putting his things on the table.*] We'd better stay up here. Harry, when my niece—when Miss Morton arrives—I want you to come and let me know. Ask her not to leave the building without seeing me.

HARRY

Yes, sir.

[*He goes out.*

FEJEVARY

Well, [*wearily*] it's been a day. Not the day I was looking for.

HOLDEN

No.

FEJEVARY

You're very serene up here.

HOLDEN

Yes; I wanted to be—serene for a little while.

FEJEVARY

[*Looking at the books.*] Emerson. Whitman. [*With a smile.*] Have they anything new to say on economics?

HOLDEN

Perhaps not; but I wanted to forget economics for a time. I came up here by myself to try and celebrate the fortieth anniversary of the founding of Morton College. [*Answering the other man's look.*] Yes, I confess I've been disappointed in the anniversary. As I left Memorial Hall after the exercises this morning, Emerson's words came into my mind—

"Give me truth,
For I am tired of surfaces
And die of inanition."

Well, then I went home—

[*Stops, troubled.*

FEJEVARY

How is Mrs. Holden?

HOLDEN

Better, thank you, but—not strong.

FEJEVARY

She needs the very best of care for a time, doesn't she?

#### HOLDEN

Yes. [*Silent a moment.*] Then, this is something more than the fortieth anniversary, you know. It's the first of the month.

#### FEJEVARY

And illness hasn't reduced the bills?

#### HOLDEN

[*Shaking his head.*] I didn't want this day to go like that; so I came up here, to try and touch what used to be here.

#### FEJEVARY

But you speak despondently of us. And there's been such a fine note of optimism in the exercises.
> [*Speaks with the heartiness of one who would keep himself assured.*

#### HOLDEN

I didn't seem to want a fine note of optimism. [*With roughness.*] I wanted—a gleam from reality.

#### FEJEVARY

To me this is reality—the robust spirit created by all these young people.

#### HOLDEN

Do you think it is robust? [*Hand affectionately on the book before him.*] I've been reading Whitman.

#### FEJEVARY

This day has to be itself. Certain things go—others come; life is change.

HOLDEN

Perhaps it's myself I'm discouraged with. Do you remember the tenth anniversary of the founding of Morton College?

FEJEVARY

The tenth? Oh yes, that was when this library was opened.

HOLDEN

I shall never forget your father, Mr. Fejevary, as he stood out there and said the few words which gave these books to the students. Not many books, but he seemed to baptise them in the very spirit from which books are born.

FEJEVARY

He died the following year.

HOLDEN

One felt death near. But that didn't seem the important thing. A student who had fought for liberty for mind Of course his face would be sensitive. You must be very proud of your heritage.

FEJEVARY

Yes. [*A little testily.*] Well, I have certainly worked for the college. I'm doing my best now to keep it a part of these times.

HOLDEN

[*As if this has not reached him.*] It was later that same afternoon I talked with Silas Morton. We stood at this window and looked out over the valley to the

lower hill that was his home. He told me how from
that hill he had for years looked up to this one, and why
there had to be a college here. I never felt America as
that old farmer made me feel it.

### FEJEVARY

[*Drawn by this, then shifting in irritation because he
is drawn.*] I'm sorry to break in with practical things,
but alas, I am a practical man—forced to be. I too have
made a fight—though the fight to finance never appears
an idealistic one. But I'm deep in that now, and I must
have a little help; at least, I must not have—stumbling
blocks.

### HOLDEN

Am I a stumbling block?

### FEJEVARY

Candidly, [*with a smile*] you are a little hard to finance. Here's the situation. The time for being a little
college has passed. We must take our place as one of
the important colleges—I make bold to say one of the
important universities—of the middle west. But we
have to enlarge before we can grow. [*Answering* HOL-
DEN's *smile*.] Yes, it is ironic, but that's the way of it.
It was a nice thing to open the anniversary with fifty
thousand from the steel works—but fifty thousand dollars—nowadays—to an institution? [*Waves the fifty
thousand aside.*] They'll do more later, I think, when
they see us coming into our own. Meanwhile, as you
know, there's this chance for an appropriation from the
state. I find that the legislature, the members who
count, are very friendly to Morton College. They like
the spirit we have here. Well, now I come to you, and

you are one of the big reasons for my wanting to put this over. Your salary makes me blush. It's all wrong that a man like you should have these petty worries, particularly with Mrs. Holden so in need of the things a little money can do. Now this man Lewis is a reactionary. So, naturally, he doesn't approve of you.

HOLDEN

So naturally I am to go.

FEJEVARY

Go? Not at all. What have I just been saying?

HOLDEN

Be silent, then.

FEJEVARY

Not that either—not—not really. But—be a little more discreet. [*Seeing him harden.*] This is what I want to put up to you. Why not give things a chance to mature in your own mind? Candidly, I don't feel you know just what you do think; is it so awfully important to express—confusion?

HOLDEN

The only man who knows just what he thinks at the present moment is the man who hasn't done any new thinking in the past ten years.

FEJEVARY

[*With a soothing gesture.*] You and I needn't quarrel about it. I understand you, but I find it a little hard to interpret you to a man like Lewis.

#### HOLDEN

Then why not let a man like Lewis go to thunder?

#### FEJEVARY

And let the college go to thunder? I'm not willing to do that. I've made a good many sacrifices for this college. Given more money than I could afford to give; given time and thought that I could have used for personal gain.

#### HOLDEN

That's true, I know.

#### FEJEVARY

I don't know just why I've done it. Sentiment, I suppose. I had a very strong feeling about my father, Professor Holden. And his friend Silas Morton. This college is the child of that friendship. Those are noble words in our manifesto:

"Morton College was born because there came to this valley a man who held his vision for mankind above his own advantage; and because that man found in this valley a man who wanted beauty for his fellow-men as he wanted no other thing."

#### HOLDEN

[*Taking it up.*] "Born of the fight for freedom and the aspiration to richer living, we believe that Morton College—rising as from the soil itself—may strengthen all those here and everywhere who fight for the life there is in freedom, and may, to the measure it can, loosen for America the beauty that breathes from knowledge." [*Moved by the words he has spoken.*]

Do you know, I would rather do that—really do that—
than—grow big.

#### Fejevary

Yes. But you see, or rather, what you don't see is,
you have to look at the world in which you find yourself.
The only way to stay alive is to grow big. It's been
hard, but I have tried to—carry on.

#### Holden

And so have I tried to carry on. But it is very hard
—carrying on a dream.

#### Fejevary

Well, I'm trying to make it easier.

#### Holden

Make it easier by destroying the dream?

#### Fejevary

Not at all. What I want is scope for dreams.

#### Holden

Are you sure we'd have the dreams after we've paid
this price for the scope?

#### Fejevary

Now let's not get rhetorical with one another.

#### Holden

Mr. Fejevary, you have got to let me be as honest
with you as you say you are being with me. You have
got to let me say what I feel.

FEJEVARY

Certainly.  That's why I wanted this talk with you.

HOLDEN

You say you have made sacrifices for Morton College.
So have I.

FEJEVARY

How well I know that.

HOLDEN

You don't know all of it.  I'm not sure you understand any of it.

FEJEVARY

[*Charmingly.*]  Oh, I think you're hard on me.

HOLDEN

I spoke of the tenth anniversary.  I was a young man
then, just home from Athens.  [*Pulled back into an old
feeling.*]  I don't know why I felt I had to go to Greece.
I knew then that I was going to teach something within
sociology, and I didn't want anything I felt about beauty
to be left out of what I formulated about society.  The
Greeks—

FEJEVARY

[*As* HOLDEN *has paused before what he sees.*]  I remember you told me the Greeks were the passion of
your student days.

HOLDEN

Not so much because they created beauty, but because
they were able to let beauty flow into their lives—to

create themselves in beauty. So, as a romantic young man, [*smiles*] it seemed if I could go where they had been—what I had felt might take form. Anyway, I had a wonderful time there. Oh, what wouldn't I give to have again that feeling of life's infinite possibilities!

FEJEVARY

[*Nodding.*] A youthful feeling.

HOLDEN

[*Softly.*] I like youth. Well, I was just back, visiting my sister here, at the time of the tenth anniversary. I had a chance then to go to Harvard as instructor. A good chance, for I would have been under a man who liked me. But that afternoon I heard your father speak about books. I talked with Silas Morton. I found myself telling him about Greece. No one had ever felt it as he felt it. It seemed to become of the very bone of him.

FEJEVARY

[*Affectionately.*] I know how he used to do.

HOLDEN

He put his hands on my shoulders. He said—"Young man, don't go away. We need you here. Give us this great thing you've got!" And so I stayed, for I felt that here was soil in which I could grow, and that one's whole life was not too much to give to a place with roots like that. [*A little bitterly.*] Forgive me if this seems rhetoric.

FEJEVARY

[*A gesture of protest. Silent a moment.*] You make it—hard for me. [*With exasperation.*] Don't you

think I'd like to indulge myself in an exalted mood?
And why don't I? I can't afford it—not now. Won't
you have a little patience? And faith—faith that the
thing we want will be there for us after we've worked
our way through the woods. We are in the woods now.
It's going to take our combined brains to get us out. I
don't mean just Morton College.

HOLDEN

No—America. As to getting out, I think you are all
wrong.

FEJEVARY

That's one of your sweeping statements, Holden.
Nobody's all wrong. Even you aren't.

HOLDEN

And in what ways am I wrong—from the standpoint
of your Senator Lewis?

FEJEVARY

He's not my Senator Lewis, he's the state's and we
have to take him as he is. Why he objects, of course,
to your radical activities. He spoke of your defense of
conscientious objectors.

HOLDEN

[Slowly.] I think a man who is willing to go to
prison for what he believes has stuff in him no college
need turn its back on.

FEJEVARY

Well, he doesn't agree with you—nor do I.

HOLDEN

[*Still quietly.*] And I think a society which permits things to go on which I can prove go on in our federal prisons had better stop and take a fresh look at itself. To stand for that and then talk of democracy and idealism—oh, it shows no mentality, for one thing.

FEJEVARY

[*Easily.*] I presume the prisons do need a cleaning up. As to Fred Jordan, you can't expect me to share your admiration. Our own Fred—my nephew Fred Morton, went to France and gave his life. There's some little courage, Holden, in doing that.

HOLDEN

I'm not trying to belittle it. But he had the whole spirit of his age with him—fortunate boy. The man who stands outside the idealism of his time—

FEJEVARY

Takes a good deal upon himself, I should say.

HOLDEN

There isn't any other such loneliness. You know in your heart it's a noble courage.

FEJEVARY

It lacks—humility. [HOLDEN *laughs scoffingly.*] And I think you lack it. I'm asking you to coöperate with me for the good of Morton College.

HOLDEN

Why not do it the other way? You say enlarge that we may grow. That's false. It isn't of the nature of

growth. Why not do it the way of Silas Morton and
Walt Whitman—each man being his purest and in-
tensest self. I was full of this fervor when you came
in. I'm more and more disappointed in our students.
They're empty—flippant. No sensitive moment opens
them to beauty. No exaltation makes them—what they
hadn't known they were. I concluded some of the
fault must be mine. The only students I reach are the
Hindus. Perhaps Madeline Morton—I don't quite
make her out. I too must have gone into a dead
stratum. But I can get back. Here alone this afternoon—[*softly*] I was back.

### FEJEVARY

I think we'll have to let the Hindus go.

### HOLDEN

[*Astonished.*]  *Go?*  Our best students?

### FEJEVARY

This college is for Americans. I'm not going to have
foreign revolutionists come here and block the things
I've spent my life working for.

### HOLDEN

I don't seem to know what you mean, at all.

### FEJEVARY

Why that disgraceful performance this morning. I
can settle Madeline all right. [*Looking at his watch.*]
She should be here by now. But I'm convinced our
case before the legislature will be stronger with the
Hindus out of here.

HOLDEN

Well, I seem to have missed something—disgraceful
performance—the Hindus, Madeline—

[*Stops, bewildered.*

FEJEVARY

You mean to say you don't know about the disturb-
ance out here?

HOLDEN

I went right home after the address. Then came up
here alone.

FEJEVARY

Upon my word, you do lead a serene life. While
you've been sitting here in contemplation I've been to
the police court—trying to get my niece out of jail.
That's what comes of having radicals around.

HOLDEN

What happened?

FEJEVARY

One of your beloved Hindus made himself obnoxious
on the campus. Giving out handbills about freedom for
India—howling over deportation. Our American boys
wouldn't stand for it. A policeman saw the fuss—came
up and started to put the Hindu in his place. Then
Madeline rushes in and it ended in her pounding the
policeman with her tennis racket.

HOLDEN

Madeline Morton did that!

FEJEVARY

[*Sharply.*] You seem pleased.

HOLDEN

I am—interested.

FEJEVARY

Well, I'm not interested. I'm disgusted. My niece mixing up in a free-for-all fight and getting taken to the police station! It's the first disgrace we've ever had in our family.

HOLDEN

[*As one who has been given courage.*] Wasn't there another disgrace?

FEJEVARY

What do you mean?

HOLDEN

When your father fought his government and was banished from his country.

FEJEVARY

That was not a disgrace!

HOLDEN

[*As if in surprise.*] Wasn't it?

FEJEVARY

See here, Holden, you can't talk to me like that.

HOLDEN

I don't admit you can talk to me as you please and that I can't talk to you. I'm a professor—not a servant.

FEJEVARY

Yes, and you're a damned difficult professor. I certainly have tried to—

HOLDEN

[*Smiling.*]   Handle me?

FEJEVARY

I ask you this.   Do you know any other institution where you could sit and talk with the executive head as you have here with me?

HOLDEN

I don't know.   Perhaps not.

FEJEVARY

Then be reasonable.   No one is entirely free.   That's naïve.   It's rather egotistical to want to be.   We're held by our relations to others—by our obligations to the [*vaguely*]—the ultimate thing.   Come now—you admit certain dissatisfactions with yourself, so—why not go with intensity into just the things you teach—and not touch quite so many other things?

HOLDEN

I couldn't teach anything if I didn't feel free to go wherever that thing took me.   Thirty years ago I was asked to come to this college precisely because my science was not in isolation, because of my vivid feeling of us as a moment in a long sweep, because of my faith in the greater beauty our further living may unfold.

[HARRY *enters.*

HARRY

Excuse me.   Miss Morton is here now, Mr. Fejevary.

FEJEVARY

[*Frowns, hesitates.*]   Ask her to come up here in five minutes.   [*After* HARRY *has gone.*]   I think we've thrown a scare into Madeline.   I thought as long as she'd been taken to jail it would be no worse for us to have her stay there awhile. She's been held since one o'clock. That ought to teach her reason.

HOLDEN

Is there a case against her?

FEJEVARY

No, I got it fixed up. Explained that it was just college girl foolishness—wouldn't happen again. One reason I wanted this talk with you first, if I do have any trouble with Madeline I want you to help me.

HOLDEN

Oh, I can't do that.

FEJEVARY

You aren't running out and clubbing the police. Tell her she'll have to think things over and express herself with a little more dignity.

HOLDEN

I ask to be excused from being present while you talk with her.

FEJEVARY

But why not stay in the library—in case I should need you. Just take your books over to the east alcove and go on with what you were doing when I came in.

HOLDEN

[With a faint smile.] I fear I can hardly do that. As to Madeline—

### FEJEVARY

You don't want to see the girl destroy herself, do you? I confess I've always worried about Madeline. If my sister had lived— But Madeline's mother died, you know, when she was a baby. Her father—well, you and I talked that over just the other day—there's no getting to him. Fred never worried me a bit—just the fine normal boy. But Madeline—[*With an effort throwing it off.*] Oh, it'll be all right, I haven't a doubt. And it'll be all right between you and me, won't it? Caution over a hard strip of the road, then—bigger things ahead.

### HOLDEN

[*Slowly, knowing what it may mean.*] I shall continue to do all I can toward getting Fred Jordan out of prison. It's a disgrace to America that two years after the war closes he should be kept there— much of the time in solitary confinement—because he couldn't believe in war. It's small—vengeful—it's the Russia of the Czars. I shall do what is in my power to fight the deportation of Gurkul Singh. And certainly I shall leave no stone unturned if you persist in your amazing idea of dismissing the other Hindus from college. For what—I ask you? Dismissed—for *what?* Because they love liberty enough to give their lives to it! The day you dismiss them, burn our high-sounding manifesto, Mr. Fejevary, and admit that Morton College now sells her soul to the—committee on appropriations!

### FEJEVARY

Well, you force me to be as specific as you are. If you do these things, I can no longer fight for you.

HOLDEN

Very well then, I go.

FEJEVARY

Go where?

HOLDEN

I don't know—at the moment.

FEJEVARY

I fear you'll find it harder than you know. Meanwhile, what of your family?

HOLDEN

We will have to manage some way.

FEJEVARY

It is not easy for a woman whose health—in fact whose life—is a matter of the best of care to "manage some way." [*With real feeling.*] What is an intellectual position alongside that reality? You'd like, of course, to be just what you want to be—but isn't there something selfish in that satisfaction? I'm talking as a friend now—you must know that. You and I have a good many ties, Holden. I don't believe you know how much Mrs. Fejevary thinks of Mrs. Holden.

HOLDEN

She has been very, very good to her.

FEJEVARY

And will be. She cares for her. And our children have been growing up together—I love to watch it. Isn't that the reality? Doing for them as best we can, making sacrifices of—of every kind. Don't let some tenuous, remote thing destroy this flesh and blood thing.

### HOLDEN

[*As one fighting to keep his head above water.*] Honesty is not a tenuous, remote thing.

### FEJEVARY

There's a kind of honesty is selfishness. We can't always have it. Oh, I used to—go through things. But I've struck a pace—one does—and goes ahead.

### HOLDEN

Forgive me, but I don't think you've had certain temptations to—selfishness.

### FEJEVARY

How do you know what I've had? You have no way of knowing what's in me—what other thing I might have been? You know my heritage; you think that's left nothing? But I find myself here in America. I love those dependent on me. My wife—who's used to a certain manner of living; my children—who are to become part of the America of their time. I've never said this to another human being—I've never looked at it myself—but it's pretty arrogant to think you're the only man who has made a sacrifice to fit himself into the age in which he lives. I hear Madeline. This hasn't left me in very good form for talking with her. Please don't go away. Just—

> [MADELINE *comes in, right. She has her tennis racket. Nods to the two men.* HOLDEN *goes out, left.*

MADELINE

[*Looking after* HOLDEN—*feeling something going on. Then turning to her Uncle, who is still looking after* HOLDEN.] You wanted to speak to me, Uncle Felix?

FEJEVARY

Of course I want to speak to you.

MADELINE

I feel just awfully sorry about—banging up my racket like this. The second time it came down on his club. Why do they carry those things? Perfectly fantastic, I'll say, going around with a club. But as long as you were asking me what I wanted for my birthday—

FEJEVARY

Madeline. I am not here to discuss your birthday.

MADELINE

I'm sorry—[*smiles*] to hear that.

FEJEVARY

You don't seem much chastened.

MADELINE

Chastened? Was that the idea? Well, if you think that keeping a person where she doesn't want to be chastens her! I never felt less "chastened" than when I walked out of that slimy spot and looked across the street at your nice bank. I should think you'd hate to —[*With friendly concern.*] Why, Uncle Felix, you look tired out.

FEJEVARY

I am tired out, Madeline. I've had a nerve-racking day.

MADELINE

Isn't that too bad? Those speeches were so boresome, and that old senator person—wasn't he a stuff? But can't you go home now and let auntie give you tea and—

FEJEVARY

[*Sharply.*] Madeline, have you no intelligence? Hasn't it occurred to you that your performance would worry me a little?

MADELINE

I suppose it was a nuisance. And on such a busy day. [*Changing.*] But if you're going to worry, Horace is the one you should worry about. [*Answering his look.*] Why, he got it all up. He made me ashamed!

FEJEVARY

And you're not at all ashamed of what you have done?

MADELINE

Ashamed? Why—no.

FEJEVARY

Then you'd better be! A girl who rushes in and assaults an officer!

MADELINE

[*Earnestly explaining it.*] But, Uncle Felix, I had to stop him. No one else did.

### FEJEVARY

Madeline, I don't know whether you're trying to be naïve—

### MADELINE

[*Angrily.*] Well, I'm *not* I like that! I think I'll go home.

### FEJEVARY

I think you will not! It's stupid of you not to know this is serious. You could be dismissed from school for what you did.

### MADELINE

Well, I'm good and ready to be dismissed from any school that would dismiss for that!

### FEJEVARY

[*In a new manner—quietly, from feeling.*] Madeline, have you no love for this place?

### MADELINE

[*Doggedly, after thinking.*] Yes, I have. [*She sits down.*] And I don't know why I have.

### FEJEVARY

Certainly it's not strange. If ever a girl had a background, Morton College is Madeline Fejevary Morton's background. [*He too now seated by the table.*] Do you remember your Grandfather Morton?

### MADELINE

Not very well. [*A quality which seems sullenness.*] I couldn't bear to look at him. He shook so.

FEJEVARY

[*Turning away, real pain.*] Oh—how cruel.

MADELINE

[*Surprised, gently.*] Cruel? Me—cruel?

FEJEVARY

Not just you. The way it passes—[*to himself*] so *fast* it passes.

MADELINE

I'm sorry. [*Troubled.*] You see, he was too old then—

FEJEVARY

[*His hand up to stop her.*] I wish I could bring him back for a moment, so you could see what he was before he [*bitterly*] shook so. He was a powerful man who was as real as the earth. He was strangely of the earth, as if something went from it to him. [*Looking at her intently.*] Queer you should be the one to have no sentiment about him, for you and he—sometimes when I'm with you it's as if—he were near. He had no personal ambition, Madeline. He was ambitious for the earth and its people. I wonder if you can realize what it meant to my father—in a strange land, where he might so easily have been misunderstood, pushed down, to find a friend like that? It wasn't so much the material things—though Uncle Silas was always making them right—and as if—oh, hardly conscious what he was doing—so little it mattered. It was the way he *got* father, and by that very valuing kept alive what was there to value. Why, he literally laid this country at my father's feet—as if that was what this country was for, as if it made up for the hard early things—for the wrong things.

### MADELINE

He must really have been a pretty nice old party. No doubt I would have hit it off with him all right. I don't seem to hit it off with the—speeches about him. Somehow I want to say, "Oh, give us a rest."

### FEJEVARY

[*Offended.*] And that, I presume, is what you want to say to me.

### MADELINE

No, no, I didn't mean you, Uncle. Though [*hesitatingly*] I was wondering, how you could think you were talking on your side.

### FEJEVARY

What do you mean—my side?

### MADELINE

Oh, I don't—exactly. That's nice about him being—of the earth. Sometimes when I'm out for a tramp—way off by myself—yes, I know. And I wonder if that doesn't explain his feeling about the Indians. Father told me how grandfather took it to heart about the Indians.

### FEJEVARY

He felt it as you'd feel it if it were your brother. So he must give his choicest land to the thing we might become. "Then maybe I can lie under the same sod with the red boys and not be ashamed."

[MADELINE *nods, appreciatively.*

MADELINE

Yes, that's really—all right.

FEJEVARY

[*Irritated by what seems charily stated approval.*] "All right!" Well, I am not willing to let this man's name pass from our time. And it seems rather bitter that Silas Morton's granddaughter should be the one to stand in my way.

MADELINE

Why, Uncle Felix, I'm not standing in your way. Of course I wouldn't do that. I—[*rather bashfully*] I love the Hill. I was thinking about it in jail. I got fuddled on direction in there, so I asked the woman who hung around which way was College Hill. "Right through there," she said. A blank wall. I sat and looked through that wall—long time. [*She looks front, again looking through that blank wall.*] It was all—kind of funny. Then later she came and told me you were out there, and I thought it was corking of you to come and tell them they couldn't put that over on College Hill. And I know Bakhshish will appreciate it too. I wonder where he went.

FEJEVARY

Went? I fancy he won't go much of anywhere to-night.

MADELINE

What do you mean?

FEJEVARY

Why, he's held for his hearing, of course.

MADELINE

You mean—you came and got just me—and left him there?

FEJEVARY

Certainly.

MADELINE

[*Rising.*] Then I'll have to go and get him!

FEJEVARY

Madeline, don't be so absurd. You don't get people out of jail by stopping in and calling for them.

MADELINE

But you got me.

FEJEVARY

Because of years of influence. At that, it wasn't simple. Things of this nature are pretty serious nowadays. It was only your ignorance got you out.

MADELINE

I do seem ignorant. While you were fixing it up for me, why didn't you arrange for him too?

FEJEVARY

Because I am not in the business of getting foreign revolutionists out of jail.

MADELINE

But he didn't do as much as I did.

FEJEVARY

It isn't what he did. It's what he is. We don't want
him here.

MADELINE

Well I guess I'm not for that!

FEJEVARY

May I ask why you have appointed yourself guardian
of these strangers?

MADELINE

Perhaps because they are strangers

FEJEVARY

Well they're the wrong kind of strangers.

MADELINE

Is it true that the Hindu who was here last year is to
be deported? Is America going to turn him over to the
government he fought?

FEJEVARY

I have an idea they will all be deported. I'm not
so sorry this thing happened. It will get them into the
courts—and I don't think they have money to fight.

MADELINE

[*Giving it clean and straight.*] Gee, I think that's
rotten!

FEJEVARY

Quite likely your inelegance will not affect it one
way or the other.

MADELINE

[*She has taken her seat again, is thinking it out.*] I'm twenty-one next Tuesday. Isn't it on my twenty-first birthday I get that money Grandfather Morton left me?

FEJEVARY

What are you driving at?

MADELINE

[*Simply.*] They can have my money.

FEJEVARY

Are you crazy? What *are* these people to you?

MADELINE

They're people from the other side of the world who came here believing in us, drawn from the far side of the world by things we say about ourselves.. Well, I'm going to pretend—just for fun—that the things we say about ourselves are true. So if you'll—arrange so I can get it, Uncle Felix, as soon as it's mine.

FEJEVARY

And this is what you say to me at the close of my years of trusteeship! If you could know how I've nursed that little legacy along—until now it is—[*Breaking off in anger.*] I shall not permit you to destroy yourself!

MADELINE

[*Quietly.*] I don't see how you can keep me from "destroying myself."

### Fejevary

[*Looking at her, seeing that this may be true. In genuine amazement, and hurt.*] Why—but it's incredible. Have I—has my house—been nothing to you all these years?

### Madeline

I've had my best times at your house. Things wouldn't have been—very gay for me—without you all —though Horace gets my goat!

### Fejevary

And does your Aunt Isabel—"get your goat?

### Madeline

I love auntie. [*Rather resentfully.*] You know that. What has that got to do with it?

### Fejevary

So you are going to use Silas Morton's money to knife his college.

### Madeline

Oh, Uncle Felix, that's silly.

### Fejevary

It's a long way from silly. You know a little about what I'm trying to do—this appropriation that would assure our future. If Silas Morton's granddaughter casts in her lot with revolutionists, Morton College will get no help from the state. Do you know enough about what you are doing to assume this responsibility?

MADELINE

I am not "casting in my lot with revolutionists." If it's true, as you say, that you have to have money in order to get justice—

FEJEVARY

I didn't say it!

MADELINE

Why you did, Uncle Felix. You said so. And if it's true that these strangers in our country are going to be abused because they're poor,—what else could I do with my money and not feel like a skunk?

FEJEVARY

[Trying a different tack, laughing.] Oh, you're a romantic girl, Madeline—skunk and all. Rather nice, at that. But the thing is perfectly fantastic, from every standpoint. You speak as if you had millions. And if you did, it wouldn't matter, not really. You are going against the spirit of this country; with or without money, that can't be done. Take a man like Professor Holden. He's radical in his sympathies—but does he run out and club the police?

MADELINE

[In a smoldering way.] I thought America was a democracy.

FEJEVARY

We have just fought a great war for democracy.

MADELINE

Well, is that any reason for not having it?

FEJEVARY

I should think you would have a little emotion about
the war—about America—when you consider where
your brother is.

MADELINE

Fred had—all kinds of reasons for going to France.
He wanted a trip. [*Answering his exclamation.*]  Why
he *said* so.  Heavens, Fred didn't make speeches about
himself.  Wanted to see Paris—poor kid, he never did
see Paris.  Wanted to be with a lot of fellows—knock
the Kaiser's block off—end war, get a French girl.  It
was all mixed up—the way things are.  But Fred was a
pretty decent sort.  I'll say so.  He had such kind,
honest eyes.  [*This has somehow said itself; her own
eyes close and what her shut eyes see makes feeling
hot.*]  One thing I do know!  Fred never went over
the top and out to back up the argument you're making
now!

FEJEVARY

[*Stiffly.*]  Very well, I will discontinue the argument
I'm making now.  I've been trying to save you from—
pretty serious things.  The regret of having stood in the
way of Morton College—[*his voice falling*] the horror
of having driven your father insane.

MADELINE

*What?*

FEJEVARY

One more thing would do it.  Just the other day I was
talking with Professor Holden about your father.  His
idea of him relates back to the pioneer life—another

price paid for this country. The lives back of him were
too hard. Your greatgrandmother Morton—the first
white woman in this region—she dared too much, was
too lonely, feared and bore too much. They did it, for
the task gave them a courage for the task. But it—left
a scar.

### MADELINE

And father is that—[*can hardly say it*]—scar.
[*Fighting the idea.*] But Grandfather Morton was not
like that.

### FEJEVARY

No; he had the vision of the future; he was robust
with feeling for others. [*Gently.*] But Holden feels
your father is the—dwarfed pioneer child. The way
he concentrates on corn—excludes all else—as if unable
to free himself from their old battle with the earth.

### MADELINE

[*Almost crying.*] I think it's pretty terrible to—wish
all that on poor father.

### FEJEVARY

Well, my dear child, it's life has "wished it on him."
It's just one other way of paying the price for this
country. We needn't get it for nothing. I feel that all
our chivalry should go to your father in his—heritage
of loneliness.

### MADELINE

Father couldn't always have been—dwarfed. Mother
wouldn't have cared for him if he had always been—like
that.

FEJEVARY

No, if he could have had love to live in. But no endurance for losing it. Too much had been endured just before life got to him.

MADELINE

Do you know, Uncle Felix—I'm afraid that's true? [*He nods.*] Sometimes when I'm with father, I feel those things near—the—the too much—the too hard,—feel them as you'd feel the cold. And now that it's different—easier—he can't come into the world that's been earned. Oh, I wish I could help him!

> [*As they sit there together, now for the first time really together, there is a shrill shout of derision outside.*

MADELINE

What's that? [*A whistled call.*] Horace! That's Horace's call. That's for his gang. Are they going to start something now that will get Atma in jail?

FEJEVARY

More likely he's trying to start something. [*They are both listening intently.*] I don't think our boys will stand much more.

> [*A scoffing whoop.* MADELINE *springs to the window; he reaches in ahead and holds it.*

FEJEVARY

This window stays closed.

> [*She starts to go away, he takes hold of her.*

### Madeline

You think you can keep me in here?

### Fejevary

Listen, Madeline—plain, straight truth. If you go out there and get in trouble a second time, I can't make it right for you.

### Madeline

You needn't!

### Fejevary

You don't know what it means. These things are not child's play—not today. You could get twenty years in prison for things you'll say if you rush out there now. [*She laughs.*] You laugh because you're ignorant. Do you know that in America today there are women in our prisons for saying no more than you've said here to me!

### Madeline

Then you ought to be ashamed of yourself!

### Fejevary

I? Ashamed of myself?

### Madeline

Yes! Aren't you an American? [*A whistle.*] Isn't that a policeman's whistle? Are *they* coming back? Are they hanging around here to—[*Pulling away from her uncle as he turns to look, she jumps up in the deep sill and throws open the window. Calling down.*] Here—Officer—*You*—Let that boy alone!

FEJEVARY

[*Going left, calling sharply.*]   Holden.   Professor Holden—here—quick!

VOICE

[*Coming up from below, outside.*]   Who says so?

MADELINE

I say so!

VOICE

And who are you talking for?

MADELINE

I am talking for Morton College!

FEJEVARY

[*Returning—followed, reluctantly, by* HOLDEN.]   Indeed you are not.   Close that window or you'll be expelled from Morton College.

[*Sounds of a growing crowd outside.*

VOICE

Didn't I see you at the station?

MADELINE

Sure you saw me at the station.   And you'll see me there again, if you come bullying around here.   You're not what this place is for!   [*Her uncle comes up behind, right, and tries to close the window—she holds it out.*]   My grandfather gave this hill to Morton College —a place where anybody—from any land—can come and say what he believes to be true!   Why you poor simp—this is America!   Beat it from here!   Atma!

Don't let him take hold of you like that! He has no right to—Oh, let me *down* there!

> [*Springs down, would go off right, her uncle spreads out his arms to block that passage. She turns to go the other way.*

### Fejevary

Holden! Bring her to her senses. Stand there. [HOLDEN *has not moved from the place he entered, left, and so blocks the doorway.*] Don't let her pass.
> [*Shouts of derision outside.*

### Madeline

You think you can keep me in here—with that going on out there?

> [*Moves nearer* HOLDEN, *stands there before him, taut, looking him straight in the eye. After a moment, slowly, as one compelled, he steps aside for her to pass. Sound of her running footsteps. The two men's eyes meet. A door slams.*

[Curtain]

## ACT THREE

SCENE: *At the* MORTON *place, the same room in which* SILAS MORTON *told his friend* FELIX FEJEVARY *of his plan for the hill. The room has not altogether changed since that day in 1879. The table around which they dreamed for the race is in its old place. One of the old chairs is there, the other two are modern chairs. In a corner is the rocker in which* GRANDMOTHER MORTON *sat. This is early afternoon, a week after the events of Act Two.*

MADELINE *is sitting at the table, in her hand a torn wrinkled piece of brown paper—peering at writing almost too fine to read. After a moment her hand goes out to a beautiful dish on the table—an old dish of colored Hungarian glass. She is about to take something from this, but instead lets her hand rest an instant on the dish itself. Then turns and through the open door looks out at the hill, sitting where her* GRANDFATHER MORTON *sat when he looked out at the hill.*

*Her father,* IRA MORTON, *appears outside, walking past the window, left. He enters carrying a grain sack, partly filled. He seems hardly aware of* MADELINE, *but taking a chair near the door, turned from her, opens the sack and takes out a couple of ears of corn. As he is bent over them, examining in a shrewd, greedy way,* MADELINE *looks at that lean, tormented, rather desperate profile, the look of one confirming a thing she fears. Then takes up her piece of paper.*

### MADELINE

Do you remember Fred Jordan, father? Friend of our Fred—and of mine?

### IRA

[*Not wanting to take his mind from the corn.*] No. I don't remember him.
> [*His voice has that timbre of one not related to others.*

### MADELINE

He's in prison now.

### IRA

Well, I can't help that. [*After taking out another ear.*] This is the best corn I ever had.
> [*He says it gloatingly, to himself.*

### MADELINE

He got this letter out to me—written on this scrap of paper. They don't give him paper. [*Peering.*] Written so fine I can hardly read it. He's in what they call "the hole," father—a punishment cell. [*With difficulty reading it.*] It's two and a half feet at one end, three feet at the other end, and six feet long. He'd been there ten days when he wrote this. He gets two slices of bread a day; he gets water; that's all he gets. This because he balled the deputy warden out for chaining another prisoner up by the wrists.

### IRA

Well, he'd better a-minded his own business. And you better mind yours. I've got no money to spend in the courts.  [*With excitement.*]  I'll not mortgage this farm!  It's been clear since the day my father's father got it from the government—and it stays clear—till I'm gone.  It grows the best corn in the state—best corn in the Mississippi Valley.  Not for *anything*— you hear me?  —would I mortgage this farm my father handed down to me.

MADELINE

[*Hurt.*]  Well, father, I'm not asking you to.

IRA

Then go and see your Uncle Felix.  Make it up with him.  He'll help you—if you say you're sorry.

MADELINE

I'll not go to Uncle Felix

IRA

Who will you go to then?  [*Pause.*]  Who will help you then?  [*Again he waits.*]  You come before this United States Commissioner with no one behind you, he'll hold you for the grand jury.  Judge Watkins told Felix there's not a doubt of it.  You know what that means?  It means you're on your way to a cell.  Nice thing for a Morton, people who've had their own land since we got it from the Indians.  What's the matter with your uncle?  Ain't he always been good to you?  I'd like to know what things would 'a been for you without Felix and Isabel and all their friends.  You want to think a little.  You like good times too well to throw all that away.

MADELINE

I do like good times. So does Fred Jordan like good times. [*Smooths the wrinkled paper.*] I don't know anybody—unless it is myself—loves to be out, as he does. [*She tries to look out, but cannot; sits very still, seeing what it is pain to see. Rises, goes to that corner closet, the same one from which* SILAS MORTON *took the deed to the hill. She gets a yard stick, looks in a box and finds a piece of chalk. On the floor she marks off* FRED JORDAN's *cell. Slowly, at the end left un-chalked, as for a door, she goes in. Her hand goes up, as against a wall; looks at her other hand, sees it is out too far, brings it in, giving herself the width of the cell. Walks its length, halts, looks up.*] And one window— too high up to see out.

> [*In the moment she stands there, she is in that cell; she is all the people who are in those cells.* EMIL JOHNSON *appears from outside; he is the young man brought up on a farm, a crudely Americanized Swede.*

MADELINE

[*Stepping out of the cell door, and around it.*] Hello, Emil.

EMIL

How are you, Madeline? How do, Mr. Morton. [IRA *barely nods and does not turn. In an excited manner he begins gathering up the corn he has taken from the sack.* EMIL *turns back to* MADELINE.] Well, I'm just from the courthouse. Looks like you and I might take a ride together, Madeline. You come before the Commissioner at four.

IRA

/What have you got to do with it?

MADELINE

Oh, Emil has a courthouse job now, father. He's part of the law.

IRA

Well, he's not going to take you to the law! Anybody else—not Emil Johnson!

MADELINE

[*Astonished—and gently, to make up for his rudeness.*] Why—father, why not Emil? Since I'm going, I think it's nice to go in with someone I know—with a neighbor like Emil.

IRA

If *this* is what he lived for! If this is why—
> [*He twists the ear of corn until some of the kernels drop off.* MADELINE *and* EMIL *look at one another in bewilderment.*

EMIL

It's too bad anybody has to take Madeline in. I should think your uncle could fix it up. [*Low.*] And with your father taking it like this—[*To help* IRA.] That's fine corn, Mr. Morton. My corn's getting better all the time, but I'd like to get some of this for seed.

IRA

[*Rising and turning on him.*] *You* get my corn? I raise this corn for you? [*Not to them—his mind now*

*going where it is shut off from any other mind.*]   If
I could make the *wind* stand still!   I want to *turn the
wind around.*

MADELINE

[*Going to him.*]   Why—father.   I don't understand
at all.

IRA

Don't understand.   Nobody understands.   [*A curse
with a sob in it.*]   God damn the wind!
                    [*Sits down, his back to them.*

EMIL

[*After a silence.*]   Well, I'll go.   [*But he continues
to look at Ira, who is holding the sack of corn shut, as
if someone may take it.*]   Too bad—[*Stopped by a sign
from* MADELINE, *not to speak of it.*]   Well, I was saying, I have to go on to Beard's Crossing.   I'll stop for
you on my way back.   [*Confidentially.*]   Couldn't you
telephone your uncle?   He could do something.   You
don't know what you're going up against.   You heard
what the Hindus got, I suppose.

MADELINE

No.   I haven't seen anyone today.

EMIL

They're held for the grand jury.   They're locked up
now.   No bail for *them.*   I've got the inside dope about
them.   They're going to get what this country can hand
'em;   then after we've given them a nice little taste of
prison life in America, they're going to be sent back
home—to see what India can treat them to.

MADELINE

Why are you so pleased about this, Emil?

EMIL

Pleased? It's nothin' to me—I'm just telling you. Guess you don't know much about the Espionage Act or you'd go and make a little friendly call on your uncle. When your case comes to trial—and Judge Lenon maybe on the bench—[*Whistles.*] He's one fiend for Americanism. But if your uncle was to tell the right parties that you're just a girl, and didn't realize what you were saying—

MADELINE

I did realize what I was saying, and every word you've just said makes me know I meant what I said. I said if this was what our country has come to then I'm not for our country. I said that—and a-plenty more—and I'll say it again!

EMIL

Well—gee, you don't know what it means.

MADELINE

I do know what it means, but it means not being a coward.

EMIL

Oh, well—Lord, you can't say everything you think. If everybody did that, things'd be worse off than they are now.

MADELINE

Once in a while you have to say what you think—or hate yourself.

EMIL

[*With a grin.*]   Then hate yourself.

MADELINE

[*Smiling too.*]   No thank you; it spoils my fun.

EMIL

Well, look-a-here, Madeline, aren't you spoiling your fun now? You're a girl likes to be out. Ain't I seen you from our place, with this one and that one, sometimes all by yourself, strikin' out over the country as if you was crazy about it? How'd you like to be where you couldn't even see out?

MADELINE

[*A step nearer the cell.*]   There oughtn't to be such places.

EMIL

Oh, well—Jesus, if you're going to talk about that—! You can't change the way things are.

MADELINE

[*Quietly.*]   Why can't I?

EMIL

Well, say, who do you think you are?

MADELINE

I think I'm an American. And for that reason I think I have something to say about America.

EMIL

Huh! America'll lock you up for your pains.

#### Madeline

All right. If it's come to that, maybe I'd rather be a locked up American than a free American.

#### Emil

I don't think you'd like the place, Madeline. There's not much tennis played there. Jesus—what's Hindus?

#### Madeline

You aren't really asking Jesus, are you, Emil? [*Smiles.*] You mightn't like his answer.

#### Emil

[*From the door.*] Take a tip. Telephone your uncle.

[*He goes.*

#### Ira

[*Not looking at her.*] There might be a fine, and they'd come down on me and take my land.

#### Madeline

Oh, no, father, I think not. Anyway, I have a little money of my own. Grandfather Morton left me something. Have you forgotten that?

#### Ira

No. No, I know he left you something. [*The words seem to bother him.*] I know he left you something.

#### Madeline

I get it today. [*Wistfully.*] This is my birthday, father. I'm twenty-one.

IRA

Your birthday? Twenty-one? [*In pain.*] Was that twenty-one years ago?
> [*It is not to his daughter this has turned him.*

MADELINE

It's the first birthday I can remember that I haven't had a party.

IRA

It was your Aunt Isabel gave you your parties

MADELINE

Yes.

IRA

Well, you see now.

MADELINE

[*Stoutly.*] Oh, well, I don't need a party. I'm grown up now.
> [*She reaches out for the old Hungarian dish on the table; holding it, she looks to her father, whose back is still turned. Her face tender, she is about to speak when he speaks.*

IRA

Grown up now—and going off and leaving me alone. You too—the last one. And—*what for?* [*Turning, looking around the room as for those long gone.*] There used to be so many in this house. My grandmother. She sat there. [*Pointing to the place near the open door.*] Fine days like this—in that chair [*points to the rocker*] she'd sit there—tell me stories of the Indians. Father. It wasn't ever lonely where father was. Then Madeline Fejevary—my Madeline came to this house. Lived with me in this house. Then one day she—walked out of this house. Through that door—through the field—out of this house. [*Bitter silence.*] Then Fred—out of this house. Now you. With Emil Johnson! [*Insanely, and almost with relief at leaving things more sane.*] Don't let him touch my corn. If he touches one kernel of this corn! [*With the suspicion of the tormented mind.*] I wonder where he went? How do I know he went where he *said* he was going? [*Getting up.*] I dunno as that south bin's locked.

### MADELINE

Oh—father!

### IRA

I'll find out. How do I know what he's doing?
> [*He goes out, turning left.* MADELINE *goes to the window and looks after him. A moment later, hearing some one at the door, she turns and finds her* AUNT ISABEL, *who has appeared from right. Goes swiftly to her, hands out.*

### MADELINE

Oh, *auntie*—I'm glad you came! It's my birthday, and I'm—lonely.

### AUNT ISABEL

You dear little girl! [*Again giving her a hug, which* MADELINE *returns, lovingly.*] Don't I know it's your birthday? Don't think that day will ever get by while your Aunt Isabel's around. Just see what's here for your birthday.

> [*Hands her the package she is carrying.*

### MADELINE

[*With a gasp—suspecting from its shape.*] Oh! [*Her face aglow.*] Why—*is* it?

### AUNT ISABEL

[*Laughing affectionately.*] Foolish child, open it and see.

> [MADELINE *loosens the paper and pulls out a tennis racket.*

### MADELINE

[*Excited, and moved.*] Oh, Aunt Isabel!—that was dear of you. I shouldn't have thought you'd—quite do that.

### AUNT ISABEL

I couldn't imagine Madeline without a racket. [*Gathering up the paper, lightly reproachful.*] But be a little careful of it, Madeline. It's meant for tennis balls.

> [*They laugh together.*

### MADELINE

[*Making a return with it.*] It's a *peach*. [*Changing.*] Wonder where I'll play now.

### AUNT ISABEL

Why you'll play on the courts at Morton College. Who has a better right?

MADELINE

Oh, I don't know. It's pretty much balled up, isn't it?

AUNT ISABEL

Yes; we'll have to get it straightened out. [*Gently.*] It was really dreadful of you, Madeline, to rush out a second time. It isn't as if they were people who were anything to you.

MADELINE

But, auntie, they are something to me.

AUNT ISABEL

Oh, dear, that's what Horace said.

MADELINE

What's what Horace said?

AUNT ISABEL

That you must have a case on one of them.

MADELINE

That's what Horace would say. That makes me sore!

AUNT ISABEL

I'm sorry I spoke of it. Horace is absurd in some ways.

MADELINE

He's a —

AUNT ISABEL

[*Stopping it with her hand.*] No, he isn't. He's a headstrong boy, but a very loving one. He's dear with me, Madeline.

MADELINE

Yes. You are good to each other.

[*Her eyes are drawn to the cell.*

AUNT ISABEL

Of course we are. We'd be a pretty poor sort if we weren't. And these are days when we have to stand to-gether—all of us who are the same kind of people must stand together because the thing that makes us the same kind of people is threatened.

MADELINE

Don't you think we're rather threatening it ourselves, auntie?

AUNT ISABEL

Why, no, we're fighting for it.

MADELINE

Fighting for what?

AUNT ISABEL

For Americanism; for—democracy.

MADELINE

Horace is fighting for it?

AUNT ISABEL

Well, Horace does go at it as if it were a football game, but his heart's in the right place.

MADELINE

Somehow, I don't seem to see my heart in that place.

AUNT ISABEL

In what place?

#### MADELINE

Where Horace's heart is.

#### AUNT ISABEL

It's too bad you and Horace quarrel. But you and I don't quarrel, Madeline.

#### MADELINE

[*Again drawn to the cell.*] No. You and I don't quarrel.

[*She is troubled.*

#### AUNT ISABEL

Funny child! Do you want us to?
[MADELINE *turns, laughing a little, takes the dish from the table, hold it out to her aunt.*

#### MADELINE

Have some fudge, auntie.

#### AUNT ISABEL

[*Taking the dish.*] Do you *use* them?—the old Hungarian dishes? [*Laughingly.*] I'm not allowed to—your uncle is so choice of the few pieces we have. And here are you with fudge in one of them.

#### MADELINE

I made the fudge because—oh, I don't know, I had to do something to celebrate my birthday.

#### AUNT ISABEL

[*Under her breath.*] Dearie!

MADELINE

And then that didn't seem to—make a birthday, so I happened to see this, way up on a top shelf, and I remembered that it was my mother's. It was nice to get it down and use it—almost as if mother was giving me a birthday present.

AUNT ISABEL

And how she would love to give you a birthday present.

MADELINE

It was her mother's, I suppose, and they brought it from Hungary.

AUNT ISABEL

Yes. They brought only a very few things with them, and left—oh so many beautiful ones behind.

MADELINE

[*Quietly.*] Rather nice of them, wasn't it? [*Her aunt waits inquiringly.*] To leave their own beautiful things—their own beautiful life behind—simply because they believed life should be more beautiful for more people.

AUNT ISABEL

[*With constraint.*] Yes. [*Gayly turning it.*] Well, now, as to the birthday. What do you suppose Sarah is doing this instant? Putting red frosting on white frosting. [*Writing it with her finger.*] Madeline. And what do you suppose Horace is doing? [*This a little reproachfully.*] Running around buying twenty-one red candles. Twenty-two—one to grow on. Big birthday cake. Party tonight.

MADELINE

But, auntie, I don't see how I can be there.

### AUNT ISABEL

Listen, dear. Now, we've got to use our wits and all pull together. Of course. we'd do anything in the world rather than see you—left to outsiders. I've never seen your uncle as worried, and—truly, Madeline, as sad. Oh, my dear, it's these human things that count! What would life be without the love we have for each other?

### MADELINE

The love we have for each other?

### AUNT ISABEL

Why, yes, dearest. Don't turn away from me, Madeline. Don't—don't be strange. I wonder if you realize how your uncle has worked to have life a happy thing for all of us? Be a little generous to him. He's had this great burden of bringing something from another day on into this day. It is not as simple as it may seem. He's done it as best he could. It will hurt him as nothing has ever hurt him if you now undo that work of his life. Truly, dear, do you feel you know enough about it to do that? Another thing: people are a little absurd out of their own places. We need to be held in our relationships—against our background—or we are —I don't know—grotesque. Come now, Madeline, where's your sense of humor? Isn't it a little absurd for you to leave home over India's form of government?

### MADELINE

It's not India. It's America. A sense of humor is nothing to hide behind!

### AUNT ISABEL

[*With a laugh.*] I knew I wouldn't be a success at world affairs—better leave that to Professor Holden. [*A quick keen look from* MADELINE.] They've driven on to the river—they'll be back for me, and then he wants to stop in for a visit with you while I take Mrs. Holden for a further ride. I'm worried about her. She doesn't gain strength at all since her operation. I'm going to try keeping her out in the air all I can.

### MADELINE

It's dreadful about families!

### AUNT ISABEL

Dreadful? Professor Holden's devotion to his wife is one of the most beautiful things I've ever seen.

### MADELINE

And is that all you see it in?

### AUNT ISABEL

You mean the—responsibility it brings? Oh, well —that's what life is. Doing for one another. Sacrificing for one another.

### MADELINE

I hope I never have a family.

### AUNT ISABEL

Well, I hope you do. You'll miss the best of life if you don't. Anyway, you have a family. Where is your father?

### MADELINE

I don't know.

AUNT ISABEL

I'd like to see him.

MADELINE

There's no use seeing him today.

AUNT ISABEL

He's—?

MADELINE

Strange—shut in—afraid something's going to be taken from him.

AUNT ISABEL

Poor Ira. So much has been taken from him. And now you. Don't hurt him again. Madeline. He can't bear it. You see what it does to him.

MADELINE

He has—the wrong idea about things.

AUNT ISABEL

"The wrong idea!" Oh, my child—that's awfully young and hard. It's so much deeper than that. Life has made him into something—something he can't escape.

MADELINE

[*With what seems sullenness.*] Well, I don't want to be made into that thing.

AUNT ISABEL

Of course not. But you want to help him, don't you? Now dear—about your birthday party—

### MADELINE

The United States Commissioner is giving me my birthday party.

### AUNT ISABEL

Well, he'll have to put his party off. Your uncle has been thinking it all out. We're to go to his office and you'll have a talk with him and with Judge Watkins. He's off the state supreme bench now—practicing again, and as a favor to your uncle he will be your lawyer. You don't know how relieved we are at this, for Judge Watkins can do—anything he wants to do, practically. Then you and I will go on home and call up some of the crowd to come in and dance tonight. We have some beautiful new records. There's a Hungarian waltz—

### MADELINE

And what's the price of all this, auntie?

### AUNT ISABEL

The—Oh, you mean—Why simply say you felt sorry for the Hindu students because they seemed rather alone; that you hadn't realized—what they were, hadn't thought out what you were saying—

### MADELINE

And that I'm sorry and will never do it again.

### AUNT ISABEL

I don't know that you need say that. It would be gracious, I think, to indicate it.

### MADELINE

I'm sorry you—had the cake made. I suppose you can eat it, anyway. I [*turning away*]—can't eat it.

### Aunt Isabel

Why—Madeline.

> [*Seeing how she has hurt her,* Madeline *goes to her aunt.*

### Madeline

Auntie, dear! I'm sorry—if I hurt your feelings.

### Aunt Isabel

[*Quick to hold out a loving hand, laughing a little.*] They've been good birthday cakes, haven't they, Madeline?

### Madeline

[*She now trying not to cry.*] I don't know—what I'd have done without them. Don't know—what I will do without them. I don't—see it.

### Aunt Isabel

Don't try to. Please don't see it! Just let me go on helping you. That's all I ask. [*She draws* Madeline *to her.*] Ah, dearie, I held you when you were a little baby without your mother. All those years count for something, Madeline. There's just nothing to life if years of love don't count for something. [*Listening.*] I think I hear them. And here are we, weeping like two idiots. [Madeline *brushes away tears,* Aunt Isabel *arranges her veil, regaining her usual poise.*] Professor Holden was hoping you'd take a tramp with him. Wouldn't that do you good? Anyway, a talk with him will be nice. I know he admires you immensely, and really—perhaps I shouldn't let you know this—sympathizes with your feeling. So I think his maturer way of looking at things will show you just the adjustment

you need to become a really big and useful person.
There's so much to be done in the world, Madeline. Of
course we ought to make it a better world. [*In a manner of agreement with* MADELINE.] I feel very
strongly about all that. Perhaps we can do some
things together. I'd love that. Don't think I'm hope-
less! Way down deep we have the same feeling. Yes,
here's Professor Holden.

> [HOLDEN *comes in. He seems older.*

### HOLDEN

And how are you, Madeline?

> [*Holding out his hand.*

### MADELINE

I'm—all right.

### HOLDEN

Many happy returns of the day. [*Embarrassed by
her half laugh.*] The birthday.

### AUNT ISABEL

And did you have a nice look up the river?

### HOLDEN

I never saw this country as lovely as it is today.
Mary is just drinking it in.

### AUNT ISABEL

You don't think the further ride will be too much?

### HOLDEN

Oh, no—not in that car.

AUNT ISABEL

Then we'll go on—perhaps as far as Laughing Creek. If you two decide on a tramp—take that road and we'll pick you up.

[*Smiling warmly she goes out.*

HOLDEN

How good she is.

MADELINE

Yes. That's just the trouble.

HOLDEN

[*With difficulty getting past this.*] How about a little tramp? There'll never be another such day.

MADELINE

I used to tramp with Fred Jordan. This is where he is now. [*Stepping inside the cell.*] He doesn't even see out.

HOLDEN

It's all wrong that he should be where he is. But for you to stay indoors won't help him, Madeline.

MADELINE

It won't help him, but—today—I can't go out.

HOLDEN

I'm sorry, my child. When this sense of wrongs done first comes down upon one, it does crush.

MADELINE

And later you get used to it and don't care.

HOLDEN

You care. You try not to destroy yourself need-lessly.

[*He turns from her look.*

MADELINE

Play safe.

HOLDEN

If it's playing safe it's that one you love more than yourself be safe. It would be a luxury to—destroy one's self.

MADELINE

That sounds like Uncle Felix. [*Seeing she has hurt him, she goes over and sits across from him at the table.*] I'm sorry. I say the wrong things today.

HOLDEN

I don't know that you do.

MADELINE

But isn't uncle funny? His left mind doesn't know what his right mind is doing. He has to think of him-self as a person of sentiment—idealism, and—quite a job, at times. Clever—how he gets away with it. The war must have been a godsend to people who were in danger of getting on to themselves. But I should think you could fool all of yourself all the time.

HOLDEN

You don't.

[*He is rubbing his hand on the table.*

MADELINE

Grandfather Morton made this table. I suppose he
and Grandfather Fejevary used to sit here and talk—
they were great old pals. [*Slowly* HOLDEN *turns and
looks out at the hill.*] Yes. How beautiful the hill
must have been—before there was a college there. [*He
looks away from the hill.*] Did you know Grandfather
Morton?

HOLDEN

Yes, I knew him. [*Speaking of it against his will.*]
I had a wonderful talk with him once; about Greece—
and the cornfields, and life.

MADELINE

I'd like to have been a pioneer! Some ways they had
it fierce, but think of the fun they had! A whole big
land to open up! A big new life to begin! [*Her hands
closing in from wideness to a smaller thing.*] Why did
so much get shut out? Just a little way back—anything
might have been. What happened?

HOLDEN

[*Speaking with difficulty.*] It got—set too soon.

MADELINE

[*All of her mind open, trying to know.*] And why
did it? Prosperous, I suppose. That seems to set
things—set them in fear. Silas Morton wasn't afraid
of Felix Fejevary, the Hungarian revolutionist. He
laid this country at that refugee's feet! That's what
Uncle Felix says himself—with the left half of his
mind. Now—the Hindu revolutionists—! [*Pause.*]
I took a walk late yesterday afternoon. Night came,

and for some reason I thought of how many nights have come—nights the earth has known long before we knew the earth.  The moon came up and I thought of how moonlight made this country beautiful before any man knew that moonlight was beautiful.  It gave me a feeling of coming from something a long way back.  Moving toward—what will be here when I'm not here.  Moving.  We seem here, now, in America, to have forgotton we're moving.  Think it's just *us*—just now.  Of course, that would make us afraid, and—ridiculous.

[*Her father comes in.*

IRA

Your Aunt Isabel—did she go away—and leave you?

MADELINE

She's coming back.

IRA

For you?

MADELINE

She—wants me to go with her.  This is Professor Holden, father.

HOLDEN

How do you do, Mr. Morton?

IRA

[*Nods, not noticing* HOLDEN'*s offered hand.*]  How 'do.  When is she coming back?

MADELINE

Soon.

IRA

And then you're going with her?

#### MADELINE

I—don't know.

#### IRA

I say you go with her. You want them all to come down on us? [*To* HOLDEN.] What are you here for?

#### MADELINE

Aunt Isabel brought Professor Holden, father.

#### IRA

Oh. Then you—you tell her what to do. You make her do it.

[*He goes into the room at left.*

#### MADELINE

[*Sadly, after a silence.*] Father's like something touched by an early frost.

#### HOLDEN

Yes. [*Seeing his opening and forcing himself to take it.*] But do you know, Madeline, there are other ways of that happening—"touched by an early frost." I've seen it happen to people I know—people of fine and daring mind. They do a thing that puts them apart— it may be the big, brave thing—but the apartness does something to them. I've seen it many times—so many times, I fear for you. You do this thing and you'll find yourself with people who in many ways you don't care for at all; find yourself apart from people who in most ways are your own people. You're many-sided, Madeline. [*Moves her tennis racket.*] I don't know about it's all going to one side. I hate to see you, so young, close a door on so much of life. I'm being just as honest with you as I know how. I myself am making compromises to stay within. I don't like it, but there are—reasons for doing it. I can't see you leave that main body without telling you all it is you are leaving. It's not a clean-cut case—the side of the world or the side of the angels. I hate to see you lose the—fullness of life.

### MADELINE

[*A slight start, as she realizes the pause. As one recalled from far.*] I'm sorry. I was listening to what you were saying—but all the time—something else was happening. Grandfather Morton, big and—oh, terrible. He was here. And he went to that walled up hole in the ground [*Rising and pointing down at the chalked cell*] where they keep Fred Jordan on bread and water because he couldn't be a part of nations of men killing each other—and Silas Morton—only he was all that is back of us, tore open that cell—it was his voice tore it open—his voice as he cried, "God damn you, this is America!" [*Sitting down, as if rallying from a tremendous experience.*] I'm sorry—it should have happened, while you were speaking. Won't you—go on?

### HOLDEN

That's a pretty hard thing to go on against. [*After a moment.*] I can't go on.

### MADELINE

You were thinking of leaving the college, and then—decided to stay? [*He nods.*] And you feel there's more—fullness of life for you inside the college than outside?

HOLDEN

No—not exactly. [*Again a pause.*] It's very hard for me to talk to you.

MADELINE

[*Gently.*] Perhaps we needn't do it.

HOLDEN

[*Something in him forcing him to say it.*] I'm staying for financial reasons.

MADELINE

[*Kind, but not going to let the truth get away.*] You don't think that—having to stay within—or deciding to, rather, makes you think these things of the—blight of being without?

HOLDEN

I think there is danger to you in—so young, becoming alien to society.

MADELINE

As great as the danger of staying within—and becoming like the thing I'm within?

HOLDEN

You wouldn't become like it.

MADELINE

Why wouldn't I? That's what it does to the rest of you. I don't see it—this fullness of life business. I don't see that Uncle Felix has got it—or even Aunt Isabel, and you—I think that in buying it you're losing it.

### HOLDEN

I don't think you know what a cruel thing you are saying.

### MADELINE

There must be something pretty rotten about Morton College if you have to sell your soul to stay in it!

### HOLDEN

You don't "sell your soul." You persuade yourself to wait.

### MADELINE

[*Unable to look at him, as if feeling shame.*] You have had a talk with Uncle Felix since that day in the library you stepped aside for me to pass.

### HOLDEN

Yes; and with my wife's physician. If you sell your soul—it's to love you sell it.

### MADELINE

[*Low.*] That's strange. It's love that—brings life along, and then it's love—holds life back.

### HOLDEN

[*And all the time with this effort against hopelessness.*] Leaving me out of it, I'd like to see you give yourself a little more chance for detachment. You need a better intellectual equipment if you're going to fight the world you find yourself in. I think you will count for more if you wait and when you strike, strike more maturely.

MADELINE

Detachment. [*Pause.*] This is one thing they do at that place. [*She moves to the open door.*] Chain them up to the bars—just like this. [*In the doorway where her two grandfathers once pledged faith with the dreams of a million years, she raises clasped hands as high as they will go.*] Eight hours a day—day after day. Just hold your arms up like this one hour then sit down and think about—[*As if tortured by all who have been so tortured, her body begins to give with sobs, arms drop, the last word is a sob.*] detachment.

[HOLDEN *is standing helplessly by when her father comes in.*

IRA

[*Wildly.*] Don't *cry*. No! Not in this house! I can't—Your aunt and uncle will fix it up. The law won't take you this time—and you won't do it again.

MADELINE

Oh, what does *that* matter—what they do to *me?*

IRA

What you crying about then?

MADELINE

It's—the *world*. It's—

IRA

The *world?* If that's all you've got to cry about! [*To* HOLDEN.] Tell her that's nothing to cry about. What's the matter with you, Mad'line? That's crazy— cryin' about the world! What good has ever come to

this nouse through carin' about the world? What
good's that college? Better we had that hill. Why is
there no one in this house today but me and you?
Where's your mother? Where's your brother? The
*world*

### HOLDEN

I think your father would like to talk to you. I'll go
outside—walk a little, and come back for you with your
aunt. You must let us see you through this, Madeline.
You couldn't bear the things it would bring you to. I
see that now. [*As he passes her in the doorway his
hand rests an instant on her bent head.*] You're worth
too much to break.

### IRA

[*Turning away.*] I don't want to talk to you. What
good comes of talking? [*In moving, he has stepped
near the sack of corn. Takes hold of it.*] But not with
Emil Johnson! That's not—what your mother died
for.

### MADELINE

Father, you must talk to me. What did my mother
die for? No one has ever told me about her—except
that she was beautiful—not like other people here. I
got a feeling of—something from far away. Something
from long ago. Rare. Why can't Uncle Felix talk
about her? Why can't you? Wouldn't she want me
to know her? Tell me about her. It's my birthday and
I need my mother.

### IRA

[*As if afraid he is going to do it.*] How can you
touch—what you've not touched in nineteen years?
Just once—in nineteen years—and that did no good.

MADELINE

Try. Even though it hurts. Didn't you used to talk
to her? Well, I'm her daughter. Talk to me. What
has she to do with Emil Johnson?

IRA

[*The pent up thing loosed.*] What has she to do
with him? She died so he could live. He lives because
she's dead. [*In anguish.*] And what is *he* alongside
her? Yes. Something from far away. Something
from long ago. Rare. How'd you know that? Find-
ing in me—what I didn't know was there. Then *she*
came—that ignorant Swede—Emil Johnson's mother—
running through the cornfield like a crazy woman—
"Miss Morton! Miss Morton! Come help me! My
children are choking!" Diphtheria they had—the whole
of 'em—but out of this house she ran—my Madeline,
leaving you—her own baby—running fast as she could
through the cornfield after that immigrant woman. She
stumbled in the rough field—fell to her knees. That
was the last I saw of her. She choked to death in that
Swede's house. They lived.

MADELINE

[*Going to him.*] Oh—father. [*Voice rich.*] But
how lovely of her.

IRA

Lovely? Lovely to leave you without a mother—
leave me without her after I'd had her? Wasn't she
worth more than them?

MADELINE

[*Proudly.*] Yes. She was worth so much that she
never stopped to think how much she was worth.

### IRA

Ah, if you'd known her you couldn't take it like that. And now you cry about the world! That's what the world is—all coming to nothing. My father used to sit there at the table and talk about the world—my father and her father. They thought 'twas all for something— that what you were went on into something more than you. That's the talk I always heard in this house. But it's just talk. The rare thing that came here was killed by the common thing that came here. Just happens— and happens cruel. Look at your brother! Gone— [*snaps his finger*] like that. I told him not to go to war. He didn't have to go—they'd been glad enough to have him stay here on the farm. But no,—he must— make the world safe for democracy! Well, you see how safe he made it, don't you? Now I'm alone on the farm and he—buried on some Frenchman's farm. That is, I hope they buried him—I hope they didn't just—[*tormented.*]

### MADELINE

Oh father—of course not. I know they did.

### IRA

How do you know? What do they care—once they got him? *He* talked about the world—better world— end war. Now he's in his grave—I hope he is—and look at the front page of the paper! No such thing— war to end war!

### MADELINE

But he thought there was, father. Fred believed that —so what else could he do?

IRA

He could 'a minded his own business.

MADELINE

No—oh, no. It was fine of him to give his life to what he believed should be.

IRA

The light in his eyes as he talked of it, now—eyes gone—and the world he died for all hate and war. Waste. Waste. Nothin' but waste—the life of this house. Why folks today'd laugh to hear my father talk. He gave his best land for ideas to live. Thought was going to make us a better people. What was his word? [Waits.]. Aspiration. [Says it as if it is a far-off thing.] Well, look at your friend young Jordan. Kicked from the college to prison for ideas of a better world. [Laughs.] His "aspiration" puts him in a hole on bread and water! So—mind your own business, that's all that's so in this country. [Constantly tormented anew.] Oh I told your brother all that—the night I tried to keep him. Told him about his mother— to show what come of running to other folks. And he said—standing right there—[pointing] eyes all bright, he said, "Golly, I think that's great!" And then he— walked out of this house. [Fear takes him.] Madeline! [She stoops over him, her arm around him.] Don't you leave me—all alone in this house—where so many was once. What's Hindus—alongside your own father —and him needing you? It won't be long. After a little I'll be dead—or crazy—or something. But not here alone—where so many was once.

MADELINE

Oh—father. I don't know what to do.

IRA

Nothing stays at home. Not even the corn stays at home. If only the wind wouldn't blow! Why can't I have my field to myself? Why can't I keep what's mine? All these years I've worked to make it better. I wanted it to be—the most that it could be. My father used to talk about the Indians—how our land was their land, and how we must be more than them. He had his own ideas of bein' more—well, what's that come to? The Indians lived happier than we—wars, strikes, prisons. But I've made the corn more! This land that was once Indian maize now grows corn—I'd like to have the Indians see my corn! I'd like to see them side by side!—their Indian maize, my corn. And how'd I get it? Ah, by thinkin'—always tryin', changin', carin'. Plant this corn by that corn, and the pollen blows from corn to corn—the golden dust it blows, in the sunshine and of nights—blows from corn to corn like a—[*the word hurts*] gift. No, you don't understand it, but [*proudly*] corn don't stay what it is! You can make it anything—according to what you do, 'cording to the corn it's alongside. [*Changing.*] But that's it. I want it to stay in my field. It goes away. The prevailin' wind takes it on to the Johnsons—them Swedes that took my Madeline! I hear it! Oh nights when I can't help myself—and in the sunshine I can *see* it—pollen —soft golden dust to make new life—goin' on to *them,* —and them too ignorant to know what's makin' their corn better! I want my field to myself. What'd I work all my life for? Work that's had to take the

place o' what I lost—is that to go to Emil.Johnson?
No! The wind shall stand still! I'll make it. I'll find
a way. Let me alone and I—I'll think it out. Let me
alone, I say.

> [*A mind burned to one idea, with greedy
> haste he shuts himself in the room
> at left. MADELINE has been stand-
> ing there as if mist is parting and
> letting her see. And as the vision
> grows power grows in her. She is
> thus flooded with richer life when
> her aunt and Professor HOLDEN
> come back. Feeling something new,
> for a moment they do not speak.*

### AUNT ISABEL

Ready, dear? It's time for us to go now

### MADELINE

[*With the quiet of plentitude.*] I'm going in with
Emil Johnson.

### AUNT ISABEL

Why—Madeline. [*Falteringly.*] We thought you'd
go with us.

### MADELINE

No. I have to be—the most I can be. I want the
wind to have something to carry.

### AUNT ISABEL

[*After a look at Professor HOLDEN, who is looking
intensely at MADELINE.*] I don't understand.

MADELINE

The world is all a—moving field. [*Her hands move, voice too is as of a moving field.*] Nothing is to itself. If America thinks so—America is like father. I don't feel alone any more. The wind has come through— wind rich from lives now gone. Grandfather Fejevary, gift from a field far off. Silas Morton. No, not alone any more. And afraid? I'm not even afraid of being absurd!

AUNT ISABEL

But Madeline—you're leaving your father?

MADELINE

[*After thinking it out.*] I'm not leaving—what's greater in him than he knows.

AUNT ISABEL

You're leaving Morton College?

MADELINE

That runt on a high hill? Yes, I'm leaving grand-father's college—then maybe I can one day lie under the same sod with him, and not be ashamed. Though I must tell you [*a little laugh*] under the sod is my idea of no place to be. I want to be a long time—where the wind blows.

AUNT ISABEL

[*Who is trying not to cry.*] I'm afraid it won't blow in prison, dear.

### Madeline

I don't know. Might be the only place it would blow. [Emil *passes the window, hesitates at the door.*] I'll be ready in just a moment, Emil.

[*He waits outside.*

### Aunt Isabel

Madeline, I didn't tell you—I hoped it wouldn't be necessary, but your uncle said—if you refused to do it his way, he could do absolutely nothing for you, not even—bail.

### Madeline

Of course not. I wouldn't expect him to.

### Aunt Isabel

He feels so deeply about these things—America— loyalty—he said if you didn't come with us, it would be final, Madeline. Even—[*breaks*] between you and me.

### Madeline

I'm sorry, auntie. You know how I love you. [*And her voice tells it.*] But father has been telling me about the corn. It gives itself away all the time—the best corn a gift to other corn. What you are—that doesn't stay with you. Then—[*not with assurance, but feeling her way.*] be the most you can be, so life will be more because you were. [*Freed by the truth she has found*] Oh—do that! Why do we three go apart? Professor Holden, his beautiful trained mind; Aunt Isabel—her beautiful love, love that could save the world if only you'd—throw it to the winds. [*Moving nearer* Holden, *hands out to him.*] Why do—[*Seeing it is not to be, she turns away. Low, with sorrow for that great beauty lost.*] Oh, have we brought mind, have we brought heart, up to this place—only to turn them against mind and heart?

### HOLDEN

[*Unable to bear more.*] I think we—must go. [*Going to* MADELINE, *holding out his hand and speaking from his sterile life to her fullness of life.*] Good-bye, Madeline. Good luck.

### MADELINE

Goodbye, Professor Holden. [*Hesitates.*] Luck to you.

> [*Shaking his head, stooped, he hurries out.*

### MADELINE

[*After a moment when neither can speak.*] Good-bye —auntie dearest. Thank you—for the birthday present—the cake—everything. Everything—all the years.

> [*There is something* AUNT ISABEL *would say, but she can only hold tight to* MADELINE'S *hands. At last, with a smile that speaks for love, a little nod, she goes.* EMIL *comes in.*

### EMIL

You better go with them, Madeline. It'd make it better for you.

MADELINE

Oh no, it wouldn't. I'll be with you in an instant,
Emil. I want to—say goodbye to my father.

> [*But she waits before that door, a door
> hard to go through. Alone, EMIL
> looks around the room. Sees the
> bag of corn, takes out a couple of
> ears and is looking at them as MADE-
> LINE returns. She remains by the
> door, shaken with sobs, turns, as if
> pulled back to the pain she has left.*

EMIL

Gee. This is great corn.

MADELINE

[*Turning now to him.*] It is, isn't it, Emil?

EMIL

None like it.

MADELINE

And you say—your corn is getting better?

EMIL

Oh, yes—I raise better corn every year now.

MADELINE

[*Low.*] That's nice. I'll be right out, Emil.

> [*He puts the corn back, goes out. From
> the closet MADELINE takes her hat*

*and wrap. Putting them on, she sees the tennis racket on the table. She goes to it, takes it up, holds it a moment; then takes it to the closet, puts it carefully away, closes the door behind it. A moment she stands there in the room, as if listening to something. Then she leaves that house.*

CURTAIN